ISBN   978-88-492-2026-1

Cover: Augmented Desk between the Department of Architecture, Sapienza Università di Roma,
and the Information Science Room of Termoli University campus, Università degli Studi del Molise – 2008.
Back cover: Augmented Desk between the Rome Aquarium, Rome Architects Association,
and the Information Science Room of Termoli University campus, Università degli Studi del Molise – 2008.

E-learning for architecture

edited by
Rosalba Belibani, Stefano Panunzi

GANGEMI EDITORE

Rosalba Belibani PhD in Architectural Composition and Theory of Architecture, is a researcher and teacher in Architectural Design at the Faculty of Architecture, Sapienza Università di Roma. Expert in information and communication technologies applied to architectural disciplines, she is responsible for LaMA_Laboratorio Multimediale di Architettura, which carries out research in the field of multimedia and e-learning for digital archiving of architectural works. Since 2007 she has been working with F. Bossalino and A. Gadola on sustainable design and environmental education.

Stefano Panunzi associate professor in Architectural and Urban Design, is expert in Information and Communication Technology. He has been professor at the Faculty of Architecture, University of Rome "La Sapienza". He has co-founded in 2005 the Faculty of Engineering in the University of Molise with specific roles for innovation in teaching and research activities. Autor and inventor of the System of Telecontiguity is now involved in Research and Development of Web Aided Design and Urban Reverse Engineering for Sustainable Green Cities.

This volume, with the E_Arch Conference and the volume "La formazione a distanza dell'Architetto" (2009) is the Research Report of PRIN 2006 "Ricerca e sperimentazione di nuovi modelli e tecnologie informatiche per la formazione a distanza dell'architetto. Research and experimental evaluation of e-learning new model and tecnologies in architecture education".
The present volume has been published with funds from the:
- Dipartimento di Scienze Animali, Vegetali e dell'Ambiente, Università degli Studi del Molise,
- Dipartimento di Progettazione Architettonica e di Disegno Industriale, Politecnico di Torino,
- Dipartimento di Architettura, Costruzioni e Strutture, Università Politecnica delle Marche.

Index

PRIN – PROGRAMMA DI RICERCA DI INTERESSE NAZIONALE 2006

MINISTERO DELL'ISTRUZIONE DELL'UNIVERSITÀ E DELLA RICERCA

Title of research programme:
RESEARCH AND EXPERIMENTATION IN NEW MODELS AND INFORMATION TECHNOLOGIES FOR THE DISTANCE TRAINING OF ARCHITECTS

Coordinator of research programme:
Lucio Valerio Barbera

Research Units taking part:

Sapienza Università di Roma
Dipartimento di Architettura
Head of research unit: Lucio Valerio Barbera

Politecnico di Torino
Dipartimento di Progettazione Architettonica e Disegno Industriale
Head of research unit: Liliana Bazzanella

Università degli Studi Roma Tre
Facoltà di Architettura
Head of research unit: Paolo Desideri

Università Politecnica delle Marche
Dipartimento di Architettura, Costruzioni e Strutture
Head of research unit: Gianluigi Mondaini

Università degli Studi del Molise
Dipartimento di Scienze Animali, Vegetali e dell'Ambiente
Head of research unit: Stefano Panunzi

Research and experimentation in new models and information technologies for the distance training of architects

AIMS OF THE RESEARCH

The principal aim of the research is to recommend and experiment a teaching method for e-learning in Architecture.

THE STRATEGIC OBJECTIVES OF THE RESEARCH PROGRAMME ARE DEFINED AS FOLLOWS:

a. The creation of on-line asynchronous interactive multimedia lessons designed to improve the multi-disciplinary dimension of architecture and to integrate design disciplines. The capacity to integrate different disciplines is the basic aim of the e-learning methods we experimented with in our research.

In the e-learning module, previously acquired experience is optimised in order to set up guidelines for the construction of e-learning tools for the training of architects, which will be published at the International Conference convened for the purpose of announcing the results of our research, and which will take place in October of this year in Rome.

b. The creation of synchronous applications which can be tried out in virtual laboratories. The chosen didactic model will be used to develop integrated self-study integrated with periods of collaborative learning thanks to the use of a virtual laboratory and a system of tele-presence.

c. The creation of thematic databases on-line as a back up to teaching and of software for the structural organisation of the multimedia material. The research will create structures to implement these online thematic databases, which will be present on the server, accessible and updateable by all users, in order to provide students with a store of well-thought out multimedia material.

d. Discovering which IT platform is best suited to the teaching of courses of architec-ture, based on the target users and the scalability of the system. The architecture hosting the teaching modules and the thematic databases which have been created independently from the different units will be resident on a server with links to storage subsystems on disc and tape, in order to ensure for every user an efficient access to the data relative to their course. The infrastructure on the e-learning platform will be distributed with remote access so that each user can have transparent access to the courses provided by the server. The platform will have a portal specifically designed to handle the entire research project and a personalisable interface allowing access to all the learning objects according to topic.

e. Experimentation with virtual laboratories of design on a high-definition 'Augmented Desk' telecontiguity platform and the use of simulation models for large scale design processes. The research will test the IT platforms and technological sets for e-learning, paying particular attention to virtual laboratories where lessons and reviews have been implemented and tried out with augmented desk technology.

f. A survey of the history of architecture from the post-war period to the sixties, to trace the origins of contemporary design. The critical hypothesis behind this survey is in fact the contention that this period is fundamental to a new design culture, which can be regarded as contemporary in that it is radically different from a modern one. The construction of the original e-learning module on the translation of this research topic.

g. The experimentation and assessment of the e-learning courses produced by the research units and the creation of a logistic structure of observation and monitoring of the effectiveness of the teaching. All the teaching modules produced by the Research Units will be tried out on a fixed number of selected students, equal to that of a traditional teaching module, and subjected to a qualitative assessment of their effectiveness. The parameters and indicators of quality will be defined, on which evaluation criteria will be based, to be used in the assessment tools evaluating the e-learning courses, both qualitatively and quantitatively.

This assessment must possess total compliance and reliability, since a comparative evaluation of learning skills will be carried out; both the students of the e-learning workshop and an equal number participating in a traditionally taught module will be evaluated equally, to estimate the real educational capabilities of the e-learning module. Anonymous questionnaires will produce an assessment score of the two types of teaching which will be one of the objective parameters for evaluating the project.

All the above objectives were, we are glad to say, successfully achieved.

DESCRIPTION OF THE RESEARCH CARRIED OUT AND THE RESULTS OBTAINED

Sapienza Università di Roma

The Research Unit of the Sapienza carried out the following activities according to the provisions of the research programme.

1. Experiments with the Moodle platform and the Wimba instrument package

Several different applications, formats and support systems were examined to find the most suitable tools for e-learning. Among these the Wimba package, available on the Moodle platform, was of interest in that it permitted the simultaneous use of interactive communication facilities such as forums, chats, blogs, and wikis, integrating them with more advanced sharing systems such as virtual classrooms, desktop sharing and application sharing, video-communication (person to person or person to group), event chronology storage and recording in a repository.

2. Application of the Moodle platform to teaching in a Combined Laboratory

We experimented with the Moodle platform as a tool in combination with traditional teaching in various courses for two consecutive academic years. The Moodle courses, used in parallel with the traditional courses, had the aim of setting up adaptive learning environments and becoming a critical-theoretical in-

strument of synthesis for the course. As well as the learning objects, course structure, course index and feedback area, which are the most well-established tools in the use of e-learning, we attempted to modify the standard functions of Moodle with other tools from other platforms. AADVD and DRL, developed by the London Architectural Association proved to be an important reference point for observing the trends in didactic production and for creating a tool for the comparative evaluation of teaching, in template rather than custom made logic. We used Flickr, a social utility network, to organise databases and websites in combination with Moodle

3. Construction and experimentation of the Telecontiguity interface, Augmented Desk, in collaboration with the RU of the Università degli Studi del Molise

Our RU collaborated in the setup of the telecontiguity augmented desk apparatus, examining the technical features of the equipment and obtaining the necessary machinery for building the system, then testing it in parallel with the Termoli RU. The telecontiguity system consists of a complex videoconferencing apparatus equipped with a special video-projector and a specially treated transparent screen. The aspects of image transmission and desktop projection have only recently been fine-tuned and the problems of scale solved, and after protracted experiments the system has achieved, and clearly demonstrated, excellent results.

4. Translation of didactic content on 'The origin of the contemporary', developed by the Roma Tre RU

The most interesting aspect of constructing the e-learning module was the translation of the research topics, previously developed by the RU of Università degli Studi Roma Tre, into learning objects for on-line teaching. The original material developed by the RU consisted of a text, an index of architects and works, a glossary and a bibliography. A grid table was devised to show the relationships between aspects of residential, urban, technological and figurative culture, both modern and contemporary. The matrix implied an access structure to the data based on images and topics. The aim was to obtain an indexed structure that was not only sequential but linear or parallel on demand. We wanted the course to be organised in a paradigm of files and to formally represent the subject of the course with its inter-disciplinary features. So the grid was transformed into an interactive diagram with direct links to chapters, topic keys and glossaries.

5. Creation of the e-learning course for an experimental workshop

For experiments in a workshop set up for the students of the fifth year of a specialist 5-year degree course in Architecture UE, we took account of the above observations on the systems to be adopted, whose objectives included:
- The creation of a 'real' lesson, devised ad hoc according to the different method of communication. Professor Desideri taught five introductory lessons on the basic topics to be navigated; the lessons were filmed at the LaMa multimedia Laboratory of Architecture and assembled in post-production to obtain files of the desired size and weighting;
- Creation of easily accessible audio/video clips and audio files capable of being downloaded on smart phones or ipods;
- Links to other contents and tools on the net (google earth, live maps, you tube, etc.) for parallel navigation and managing of basic traditional behaviours transferred into digital actions on the web;
- Entries into the glossary of new contents on the part of the students, to activate interaction;
- Transmission of live teaching events to a wide audience;
- The use of other tools to improve interaction between participants;
- Capture screens of recordings destined for the repository.

All the text glossaries and iconographic menus belonging to the course were placed in the 'Reference' block. We also created a topic-organised database that could be implemented by both teachers and students, where each new item was automatically linked to the course contents In the resources blocks, also, a classification of web resources available on the net was added to *Tools and facilities for teaching*, plus technological inputs, organised in the form of glossaries, containing a brief description and the relative URL. In identifying and grouping these tools and facilities we took account of the different stages of the process of collaboration to which corresponded specific tools named for specific actions.
http://elearning.uniroma1.it/course/view.php?id=999

6. Monitoring the students' activities

In order to be able trace as far as possible the students' navigation, the subjects being taught were packaged as autonomous 'resources'. By using logs (chronological record of operations and the file names where the records are memorised) we could gain information on the students' individual navigation paths, allowing us to evaluate the acceptability and didactic effectiveness of the various resources. Comparing the logs of every student also helped us to draw up statistical assessments of the various modes of access to and methods of consulting the e-learning contents.

7. Evaluation of data, in collaboration with the RU of the Polytechnic of the Marche

We evaluated the students' activities in the following ways:
- The compilation of a questionnaire ex ante (level of knowledge of the topics before the course);
- Monitoring the activities of the students as they progressed on the course;
- The compilation of a questionnaire ex post (the level of knowledge obtained by the student);

Monitoring the logs, which allowed us to assess: access to the course, times and frequencies. The data was transferred to graphs and histograms which showed the frequency of visits on a weekly basis and the average of trend of accesses, while the analysis of the logs allowed us to evaluate the preferences.

8. Conclusions and redefinition of guidelines

In conclusion, although the interface did not give the platform full formal adaptability in line with the specific contents, its limits were compensated by a series of back-up tools which were easy to implement, such as:
- Handing in of tasks or worksheets by the students;
- Automatic organisation of the activities in chronological order;
- Automatic activation of 'key words' linked to all the material in the glossaries;
- Monitoring by means of logs of the students' performance on the course;
- Forums, chat and more advanced interaction tools such as wimba.

In the light of the experience gained over the last year, the RU redefined the guidelines for constructing the module and published a short technical manual. The methods for link-up/ downloading and the tools for destination/use of the multimedia contents allowing the use of e-learning without any impediment of time or place can be found in: podcasting, mp3 readers, Ipods, blueberries, smartphones, and laptops with wireless connection.

Politecnico di Torino

The RU examined in detail the methods and experimentation of Virtual Laboratories for large scale design: The research had two main objectives.

1. Design research

Central to the project was the structuring of the work and the experiments carried out. The planning of topics, even more than the didactic-oriented features, was explored by applying transformation hypotheses to actual cases of design under study, experimented through telecontiguity, in around twenty international sessions and design workshops. At the same time the RU worked on the organisation of methodologies. As far as the method was concerned, a patchwork of roles and teacher-student interactions was imagined, especially when created by means of telecontiguity. The separate categories were open to the teachers and students who participated in the various experiments of our own and other RUs. The method of study was rendered particularly open and accessible by the use of a software system as support for both analysis and workshop activities.

2. Support software for teaching design

The RU developed software for the semantically structured organisation of the multimedia material used in the project. The system is easy and straightforward to use; both the work produced by the students and the teacher-student interaction are mainly put into practice by ICT. The method can be summarised in the definition of its semantic levels, their categorisation, and the analysis of semantically similar units in the multimedia material housed in the system, and the real semantically structured organisation of the multimedia units.

The method is put into practice using software supporting the definition of the semantic levels, both of the units themselves and their structural organisation. The RU tried out the software, creating the index-linking of the remote interactions and the project work carried out on the topic of urban transformation. As an example, one of the semantically organised structures was divided into three sections: Architecture, Design, and Communication/collaboration process. Each of these had values:

- *Architecture*: open public space, monumentality, environmental sustainability;
- *Design*: knowledge, inspection, work, finishing;
- *Communication/collaboration process*: task management, team working, decision making.

The subdivisions could be carried further; in that 'open public space' could contain further subclasses within it. Some values could be structured temporally and be described chronologically.

As a tool for validating the method and the system, the software can automatically generate narrative flows which assemble the multimedia units, by indicating the semantic categories of subjective interest. Some examples of these narrative flows can be found in video format at

http://frigo.polito.it:8080/grid/temp/Beijing-Torino_design_studio.avi

Università degli Studi Roma Tre

Our research surveyed the period in the history of architecture from the end of the Second World War to the sixties in order to pinpoint the origins of contemporary design culture. The critical idea at the basis of this survey is that this period saw the foundation of a new design culture, considered to be contemporary in that it is radically different from the modern culture. The period, crucial for our understanding of current orientations in architecture, has been dismissed by critics and historians as a final decadent phase of the Modern Movement, compared to the twenties when the historical European avant-garde played centre-stage.

In order to highlight the diverse implications of a radically novel approach to doing architecture and to its cultural context, five main themes were investigated: living space culture, urban culture, representational culture, building culture and design culture.

1. A new living-space culture

From the modern standard to the individual scale of contemporary living-space

1.1 Living-space according to the Modern Movement

The features of the modern living-space culture include an emphasis on certain aspects such as collective scale, the idea of the standard, the *existenzminimum*, the rational and functional approach gauged to the needs of the working class.

1.2 Living-space culture at the origins of the contemporary

In the fifties a new living-space culture developed in the USA, as can be seen from the media and especially from the advertising of the time: the house embodied dreams, aspirations, comfort and well-being, which from the end of the war were no longer the same but took on radically different forms.

2. A new urban culture

The idea of the functional city for industrial civilisation replaced by an urban model where functions are widely scattered

2.1 The urban culture for the Modern Movement: a city that is functional, from the level of single houses to that of the entire city; the Modern Movement sees the city as the result of a linear process from the housing cell unit upwards.

2.2 The model of the campus and the suburban production centre

The new idea of the city focuses on a living-space culture involving private mobility.

3. A new building culture

From building sites organised for works to the introduction of industrial products to be assembled off-work

3.1 Building culture according to the Modern Movement

Architectural debate in Europe during the twenties and thirties focused on introducing industrial procedures and technologies into building construction, by means of standardisation and prefabrication.

3.2 Building culture at the origins of the contemporary

In post-war American building construction culture systems were propagated that involved frameworks set with panels giving more flexibility, spatial apertures and transparency, more adapted to the informal lifestyle of the post-war years.

4. A new representational culture

From art and media for a society of mass consumption to that of a society of individual mass consumption

4.1 The elitist concept of artworks embraced by the Modern

Modern art operates at a reduced level compared to the past, declaring itself to be elitist art. Along with modern architecture it begins to make distinctions between activities that resolve practical needs and those that serve cultural requirements.

4.2 The artwork as opposed to the everyday, the banal, the serial industrial product

Production in series means standardisation of products and of mass consumption, engendering a completely new aesthetics and commercialisation of culture.

5. A new design culture

From the architect as author to the multidisciplinary team

5.1 Design culture according to the Modern Movement: the reduction of existing variables

Until the fifties engineering issues were subordinated to the logic of architecture and the best results were obtained by optimising the few existing variables.

5.2 Design culture at the origins of the contemporary: the governance of complex systems

From the fifties onwards, an ever-increasing number of variables enter the picture and the complexities arising from technological issues necessitate a redefinition of the relationship between architecture and engineering.

Università Politecnica delle Marche

The Ancona RU created a series of multimedia interactive lessons with supporting thematic databases for the purpose of evaluating the effectiveness of e-learning in architecture.

Architectural Design is a difficult subject to teach as it involves more complex cognitive activities. Our RU identified four main critical aspects in the construction of e-learning modules for architecture:

- Teaching in architecture and in engineering is principally focused on the Process of Design, with a strong emphasis on the 'professional' nature of the project.
- The main problems for the students arising from the use of teaching materials currently available on-line are knowledge overload, disorientation, distraction and the diminishing of narrative and conceptual flow. Students involved in e-learning need assistance in tracing and assessing the information on-line.
- Sometimes on-line courses run the risk of 'flattening out', from the lack of semantics and conceptual correlations that a machine is not capable of providing.
- Criteria and methods have not yet been

clearly defined for evaluating the effectiveness of e-learning methods in different educational contexts in the case of various e-learning models for architecture such as self-study, scaffolding or life-long learning. Our work in overcoming these critical aspects was divided into four stages.

1. Learning processes

An investigation was made into the kinds, roles and structures of the knowledges needed to support learning processes in the teaching of architectural design.

2. Knowledge structure

The second stage involved defining a knowledge structure that could be coherently implemented by every teacher, and which would bring about the hoped-for process models by means of navigation among the concepts and materials inserted by the teachers. The database gave the students the opportunity to acquire design experience through a personalised theme-based navigation which at the same time implanted critical and multi-disciplinary capacities.

3. Pilot lessons

Two pilot lessons were planned as a mockup for the technological development of the assumed e-learning method, with the aim of showing how it was possible, and simple, to organise strongly interconnected on-line lessons using predetermined knowledge structures. All the contents of the database were given a descriptive label, indexed and linked to demarcated glossaries.

4. Evaluation protocols

A protocol was determined for the experimental evaluation of the effectiveness of the e-learning methods and tools that were developed by the RU of Rome Sapienza.

The evaluation of the results of the experiments has two aims:
- The evaluation of the e-learning tool by comparing it with traditional methods of teaching.
- An appraisal of how far the tool came up to expectations, by analyses and evaluation of the learning processes.

We used three forms of evaluation:
- Of the students' learning, by a pre-questionnaire;
- Of the tools used by the students;
- Of the effective interaction between system and user by using the system logs.

The data was statistically correlated according to the following evaluation objectives: the level of learning, the functioning of the tool, the usability and effectiveness of use of the system.

Università degli Studi del Molise

Only at the end of our research did our RU attain the objectives that we had set ourselves – HD and overprinted graphics, the simulation of which was shown during the conference held by our research network PRIN 2006. After the critical testing stage of the performance limitations of various screen solutions, we felt that investment in videoconferencing apparatus and real-time digital manipulation was justified. In the second year other research fronts were opened:
- Passage to HD videoconference data transmission. A basic initial apparatus was acquired for the first tests, and its twin by the Rome Sapienza RU, which had excellent results and led to the donation of a HD terminal to each campus of the Università degli Studi del Molise;
- experimentation with mixer systems in real time, with standard HD, for the superimposure in croma-key of desktop graphics on videoconferences. In this case we bought a mixer console for each HD (as did Rome Sapienza RU), adapted to also support the DualVideo signal of the videoconference;
- feasibility of automatic matching systems in the two triads: telecamera-videoprojector-screen intersected at a distance by the two connected terminals. Reciprocal manual matching between the capture and projection frames intersecting between the two terminals was a crucial problem, complicated by the high number of optical variables in play. The automatic matching was resolved by resorting to algorithmic programming, carried out by Dr Giovanni Avanzi. The specific topic of his research activity was "the feasibility analysis of hardware and software solutions for the automatic calibration of digital broadcasting in videoconferencing".
- feasibility of interactive wireless peripherals compatible with any type of software application. The recent developments in wireless peripherals for playstations and the deregulation of software for development gave us the idea of using this sort of interaction on the telecontiguity surface. Daniele Pellegrini, expert in "the feasibility analysis of hardware and software solutions for shared interactivity on 3D models in videoconferencing" showed the feasibility of programming

plug-ins for any type of application. The miniaturisation of the system was made possible thanks to the arrival on the market of new models of micro- and pico- LED video projectors and the intensification of mobile telephone bands for data transmission. For this purpose a three-year convention was stipulated with H3G SpA (provider 3 of mobile phones) for the development of a portable miniaturised telecontiguity system. The interest aroused by this invention has led to the Università degli Studi del Molise being joined by other Italian partners outside the university circuit in a Scientific Experimentation Network, which was created thanks to this research. We hope this will lead to spin-offs for future pubic services of excellence as well as industrial patenting.

Problems encountered during the research

During the research we came across problems that were usually of a strictly technical nature, such as the application of the e-learning modules into the chosen platforms and the numerous problems connected with the creation of the telecontiguity prototype, Augmented Desk. Consequently the more serious difficulties were found in the specifically technological activities of the Rome Sapienza and Università degli Studi del Molise Research Units.

Sapienza Università di Roma

The Moodle platform for e-learning
While it presented no problems as far as accessibility and interactivity were concerned, the platform did not fully meet the requirements of personalised programming. Particularly, the interface structure was found to be somewhat inflexible, perhaps because of its all-inclusive applicability, which in its original design made it difficult to be adapted linguistically and formally to the type of course (SSD) or to a learning method capable of being personalised.

While constructing the course we found that in positive terms the platform was suitable for the use of didactic modules according to certain requirements such as the level of interactivity, the target users and the scalability of the system, in anticipation of a level of use involving only a few dozen people in direct simultaneous access, but which was now expected to involve a large number of experimentation groups at the same time. The limitations of Moodle were also found

in other specific requirements of the teaching of design: the need to read CAD files and make corrections directly on the files. A number of other surveys of the features of alternative software packages, both commercial and open-source showed that this inflexibility was shared by many. In the case of Moodle, Rome Sapienza has, at our suggestion, officially set up an experimental programme entrusted to a team of software designers; we await Moodle 2, into which the adaptations that we tried out and requested should be included. In the applications for dissertation seminars, furthermore, for reasons of flexibility it was decided to give all the participants, whether teachers or students, the role of 'teachers'; this was the only way for everyone to take part with equal roles, have the authority to explore the platform, upload external resources and, much more importantly, be able to compare their work with that of the others involved.

Università degli Studi del Molise

Telecontiguity, Augmented Desk
The objectives simulated during the conference held by our Research Network PRIN 2006 (Turin, Ancona, Rome Sapienza, Roma Tre and Termoli) were only achieved at the end of our research after we solved the problems inherent in HD, the superimposed graphics and the collimation. Once we passed the critical stage of testing the performance states of various alternative solutions for the screens, we felt we were justified in investing in videoconferencing apparatus and digital real-time manipulation. In the second year we addressed the following problems:
- Passage to HD videoconferencing data transmission. Basic initial apparatus was acquired for the first tests (Rome Sapienza/Molise), which had excellent results;
- experimentation with mixer systems in real time, with standard HD, for the superimposure in croma-key of desktop graphics on videoconferences. In this case we thought it necessary to acquire a control mixer for each HD (Rome Sapienza/Molise), adapted to also support the DualVideo signal;
- auto-collimation systems in the two triads: telecamera-videoprojector-screen intersected at a distance by the two connected terminals. Reciprocal manual matching between the capture and projection frames at the two terminals was a crucial problem, complicated by the high number of optical variables in play, but this was resolved by resorting to algorithmic programming.

Introduction

INFORMATION SCIENCE AND DEMOCRACY

E-learning, education at a distance using computer technology, plays a integral part in the democratic expansion of university education which, after the end of the Second World War, gathered momentum both in theory and practice in the USA, where, alongside the traditional – and for us extremely modern – possibility of choosing the place and the quality of one's own education, a choice made practicable by the great mobility of the student population, the universities began to address themselves to the less mobile section of the population, which was settled in less developed areas all over the country. This meant attempting to reach enormous numbers of people who both as a class and as individuals were socially, economically or culturally underprivileged, and who, as their mobility decreased, were forced to resort to lower and lower levels of secondary education, consisting, in the better cases, of Teaching Colleges and Junior Colleges. This mass of people was looking for some form of intermediate technical education or often was trying to regain levels of technical ability and culture that they had lost during years of unskilled labour or during military service in the vast armies that the US deployed at the end of the war. Also, there was a strong impetus to improve their technical skills on the part of individuals who, whatever their age, against the backdrop of the great wave of economic optimism that was a feature of the post-war years, were determined to climb the social ladder by acquiring the most up-to-date or exhaustive specialist skills. After a first stage marked by several if sporadic local initiatives, backed by the humanitarian spirit so typical of American society, the experts of the American University, foremost among them Clark Kerr[1], offered a coherent solution, as an ideal or rather an ideological and political response, to the problem of the variety of educational itineraries offered by the universities. Necessity and the novel experiments already underway gave them an excellent opportunity to think long and hard on the role and the meaning of a University in a mass society; in other words, in a society intricately and variously structured, in which, openly or latently, there existed an ever-growing demand for a form of education that the 'traditional' university system could not meet without undergoing a comprehensive and convincing reform. It was Clark Kerr in his famous book *The Uses of the University* in 1963 who put forward the idea that the university in its classic sense no longer existed. The time was right, perhaps, for such an idea. The debate on the role of the modern university in Britain and America had already lived through two cardinal moments: one halfway through the nineteenth century in the writings of John Henry Newman[2], and the other in the first half of the twentieth with Abraham Flexner[3].

---

[1] Clark Kerr (1911-2003) was the first chancellor of the University of California, Berkeley, and the twelfth president of the University of California. He is regarded as the acknowledged expert on the American university in its transformations in the second half of the twentieth century, and the recognised master of all those who contributed to the changes in methods and applications and to the great increases in participation in education and improvements in university management in the USA.

[2] John Henry Newman (1801-1890) was a pre-eminent figure in British academic and religious circles in the nineteenth century. He was a teacher at Oxford. Ordained as an Anglican priest, his subsequent conversion to Catholicism was much commented on at the time.

[3] Abraham Flexner (1866-1959), physician and educator, founded the Institute for Advanced Study at Princeton.

In their ideas and works these two masters moved away from the idea of a University as a community of scholars dedicated to knowledge for its own sake – and thus favouring a non-specific education, that of undergraduates rather than graduates – towards a concept of the University as a place of instruction where high-level professionals, the embodiment of the ruling classes, would be trained by a specialised, scientific and technological educational system. Flexner, the American, was particularly absorbed with the sense of leadership that the University had to instil not only into the classes destined to govern the country, but also – and above all – into the entire society. "Universities must give to society not what society wants, but what it needs". This was the lynchpin of Flexner's teaching, and to this day certain great American universities hold true to his concept, or would like to. But in the fifties and sixties the world had changed and society was questioning their countries' leaderships, and thus also the university system, with the vehemence typical of mass behaviour and the passion of political urgency. Clark Kerr held his most responsible posts at the University of Berkeley and the University of California at the same time as the struggle for Civil Rights and of the Free Speech Movement, the anti-Vietnam War protests and the first wave of Baby Boom youth who were pounding on the doors of the universities to be let in to claim their right to higher education. Kerr, an economist with a clear sense of history and also of politics, like some prophet had already understood at the end of the fifties that the universities, as he put it, were 'at a junction of history'; anchored firmly in their past, they appeared to be floating uncertainly towards a future that was difficult to perceive. Today David Ward, president of the American Council on Education is right in saying that "every student and every head of university owes to Clark Kerr a great debt of gratitude – because it was his vision, courage and determination that led to the creation of the modern university and to the idea that every student, whatever their background, had the right to enter a university college". The new University, born in California, became a model and a 'realisable objective' for numerous American institutions of higher education; it was conceived of as a collection of communities: the community of the undergraduates and of the graduates; the community of the humanists, of the scientists and of the social scientists; the community of the purely professional faculties, of the non-academic personnel, and of the administrators. This cluster of communities, of often conflicting interests, was supplemented by other communities outside the university, from that of the former students to that of the representatives of various levels of government, to the communities at a local level, groups of financiers, foundations, non-government organisations. At a time when political action on the part of the students was becoming the most powerful and dynamic aspect of university dialectics and against which all reforms had to be measured, even the mobile student communities began to play a full, if often fickle, part in the new University.

Certainly, one cannot compare the dynamic events taking place on American campuses in those crucial years with the upheavals happening in Italian universities in the same period. The social and ideological impetus towards the right of access to university was just as strong in Italy, if slightly behind the American experience, at the end of the sixties and throughout the seventies. What was lacking was a bold coherent idea of the energy of reform like that which in California - the true national laboratory of America – was involving teachers and thinkers, important university administrators and interested politicians. However, the new American university, whose influence extended to almost all levels of society, represented the most coherent and rapid response to changes in a society that was in no way comparable to Italian society, either from the socio-political or cultural point of view. In Italy no one was prepared to turn a time of intense crisis into an opportunity for increasing the genuine benefits that the University could bring to the entire country, as well as to its own system; in America the benefits amounted to impressive advances in research, a substantial improvement in the quality of life for a large section of society, greater efficiency in university institutions, a higher social status for members of the scientific community, leading to their increased influence on political decision-making, as well as – what could perhaps could have been easily achieved also in Italy – a higher level of service towards the public bodies and communities of the areas in which the universities were located. All this, however, was beyond the practical, or even cultural, capabilities of the scientific and political power holders in Italian universities, even the best of them. Yet long before the onset of the deep social upheavals that shook Italian universities after 1968, when word and proof of the great programmatic advances gaining ground across the Atlantic reached Italy, it was immediately understood that the movement of ideas of which Clark Kerr was the chief, though not the only, instigator, included as their pivotal component the comprehension of the importance, for any reform to be successful, of the widest possible use of all the means of communication and information available at the time. Already in 1964, it was not uncommon to hear in the classrooms and debates in the Italian University strong appeals to the new experiences taking place in America, where "the University is on the move and branching out, multiplying its institutions at a local level, expanding them by adapting to the needs of the area, reaching even inside people's homes with its radio and TV programmes... one therefore begins to perceive that there exists a kind of *Invisible University*, which, using the idea Mumford adopted for the entire city, emerges wherever certain functions that require the physical presence of all the participants are replaced by functions that can be discharged by reproduction by mechanical means, electronic transmission and rapid distribution to anywhere on the planet... One is struck by the fact that perhaps a more modern University can blend into a more modern city just when it loses its firm outlines and the strict physical contiguity of its structures and begins to reflect in its own progress what is taking place territorially and technologically in the city as a whole. This new idea of a technologically evolved university, integrated into enormous areas where there is not only a multiplicity of possible choices but also of means of access and where competition, selection and specialisation, and also social density can reach a maximum, has been given in America a new name: the *Multiversity*."[4] The writer of this passage had in mind the lessons that Clark Kerr had given the year before as President of the University of California, in which, for his idea of a new university, he coined this expressive term, Multiversity; the writer could certainly deduce the importance and cultural roots of this intricate concept – the reference to Mumford shows this - but he could also accept it as an element that

was perfectly transferrable into the Italian context, especially, or entirely, as regarded the role played by new – or not so new – information technologies in the expression and fulfilment of the social and scientific objectives of the Multiversity.

This was still a long time before the spread of the personal computer, but there is nothing surprising in the fact that, in the above quote, along with 'reproduction by mechanical means' one could already talk of 'electronic transmission'. The computer revolution and its personalisation was already in the air. In October 1965, at the Bema Show in New York, what is considered to be the first ever Personal Computer, the Olivetti Programma 101, was unveiled; an incredible missed opportunity for Italian industry. We had to wait another ten years for the Altair 8800 (January 1975), twelve for the renowned Commodore Pet (January 1977). In that same year, however, the Apple II (June 1977 came on the market, which marked the turning point that the scientific and educational world was waiting for, and began the production of the first generation of PC's which lasted from 1977 to 1985, in other words until the evolution of electronics decisively moved in the direction which brought the performance of so called home computers close to that of professional workstations.

Already in December 1968, Douglas Englebart, an American researcher at the Stanford Research Institute, in a demonstration – later dubbed 'the Mother of all demonstrations' – held at the Fall Joint Computer Conference (FJCC) in the San Francisco Convention Center, had foreshadowed all the scientific and educational developments that would be stimulated by widespread use of computers. Putting into effect the research carried by his group – the Augmentation Research Center of SRI International – he constructed for the occasion a network of a thousand professional stations spread over a vast area, and put into effect – and practice – clearly and brilliantly what would have been a normal working day in front of a computer in the twenty-first century: introducing interactive texts, videoconfer-

---

[4] Lucio Barbera, 'L'Architettura dei Campus universitari in America', lesson given during the course of Architectural Composition B in the academic year 1964-65 (course professor Ludovico Quaroni). Course Topic: 'A new University campus for Rome'.

encing, tele-conferences, e-mail, hypertext and the use of the mouse, of which he was the inventor. In other words he demonstrated the extraordinary potential of what he himself called NLS, or oNLine System.

Today in America it is virtually commonplace to express regret that the principles underlying the Multiversity, in the long run, and because of the spread of a large variety and different levels of universities, have led to a flagging of attention paid to a coherent basic intellectual education, and to an excessive misuse of specialisation and the fragmentation of knowledge. Undoubtedly the conflict of interest between those who are bent on working for the aims of research and those who believe in its commercialisation has created often serious distortions in direction both of research itself and of education. Additionally, competition within the galaxy of higher education has often ruined any conditions for collaboration or partnerships between universities. In fact, even those who believed that opening the doors and windows of the universities would lead to an increase in community spirit, are now complaining of the loss of any sense of academic community, whether humanistic or scientific. At any rate, as an inalienable part of our common heritage there remains the growing contribution made by information science to the effectiveness and efficiency of research, to the collaboration between great networks of participants, to the spread of knowledge and to the reliability of results. What we would like to say is that there remains information science's contribution to the democratisation of education, which was one of the original prophetic suppositions of the Multiversity. In practice, and not only in Europe, there is still much to be done, and above all, to debate. In fact, in view of recent experiences and partial disappointments, it seems more appropriate to thoroughly reconsider this mission that information science is supposed to be embarked upon; society, and not only American society, has undergone further changes. Just as the borders between classes and between the political parties that represented them have been removed, the idea that there is a clean division between those who can and those who cannot participate, directly and physically, in academic activity in educational establishments is no longer true; or at least it is no longer completely tenable. Apart from cases at either extremity of the scale – i.e. those people who devote themselves to their studies with all the means, and time, at their command on the one hand, and those on the other who encounter serious obstacles to devoting themselves even partially – we are dealing with a demand for an education in which most people, during the time spent in university studies, at least in certain period, show only a partial willingness to move around and, shocking as it may seem, only a partial interest in the education on offer (either from reasons of work or because in many cases the opportunities for education that non-academic society offers, knowingly or unconsciously, are numerous, attractive and even advisable). It may be better, therefore, to think of the NLS mainly as a resource which is also only partially usable for educational purposes, to be integrated into, but not to replace, the activities carried out in the places specifically set aside for them.

There is however a second reason why we should reconsider the mission of information science in university education. The 'democratisation' of university entrance in the last few decades, even in Italy, has led to academic institutions taking on the character of mass educational establishments. All the educational organisations of the first and second level have been, and still are, subjected to great pressures; one need only look at the size some of the bigger universities have attained – for example, Rome Sapienza in forty years has grown from around thirty thousand students to around a hundred and fifty thousand. This vast increase in student numbers has not been accompanied by a proportional growth in the number of teachers, and when the student-teacher ratio has been maintained, the necessary quality of the teaching has suffered, for the simple reason that research, where teaching quality is created, has not been able to increase to the same extent as the teaching, either in terms of suitable personnel or in terms of financing. The institution of the university is nowadays very different, in the way it functions, from the university whose formal structure it still replicates. In any case, that unique and indispensible straightforward rapport between teachers and students that took place during lessons but above all in other complementary moments of university life, where students had access to their professors, where they could converse and collaborate, is not practicable or even feasible in the new mass university. We should, therefore, be designing and experimenting with new forms of teacher-student relations, where, for example, a large part of the basic ideas could be taught electronically, personalised if possible, while the time for 'face-to-face interaction' between students and teachers could become the principal part of the educational process, taking place in un-mediated dialogue between the 'master' and the 'pupil'. We need to completely rethink the system of how the teaching is distributed, breaking it up into different stages; today it is in fixed hours of lessons and laboratory; we have to move on to more flexible, and above all more dependable, systems where the main burden of information is presented to the students on-line, while the physical presence of teachers and students together or their participation in laboratory work is reserved for the more important parts of the teaching programme where the teacher is irreplaceable. Naturally every discipline, every educational itinerary will have, as it does today, its own specific objectives, methods and difficulties that must be surmounted; but in general one can say that throughout the entire sector there is a real need for a commitment to a radical structural reform of the didactic system and the ways in which the students and teachers can participate in it. Of course, one presumes that a different function of on-line information will correspond to the three educational levels, from the three-year degree to the doctorate; at the first levels the e-learning can mostly replace traditional teaching, while at higher levels the computer tools will be increasingly used for advanced learning and proper research activities.

There is a third point worthy of consideration. The growth of universities has been paralleled by a multiplication of separate research and educational groups with their own specific qualities, attitudes, and 'philosophies' which has led to a thinning out of particularly brilliant scientific personalities, meagrely spread out as they are in a constellation of perhaps too many components. The capacity of the oNLine System to catalyse research and education on the web seems to point the way towards the development of the students' learning paths, especially of those at the second or third level, by the addition of shared experience between different centres and students with different training and different basic cultures, given the fact that the NLS by its very nature ignores national boundaries. This becomes particularly interesting in our case where peripheral centres are willing to connect up to the historical central group of institutions that makeup the Italian university system, by creating access to centres of higher educational quality, beginning with decentralised institutions. One can definitively maintain, therefore, that within a consciously reformed environment, the use of NLS as tool for sharing high-level educational experience, even in cases of on-line relations between groups belonging to universities possessing identical qualifications, can decisively increase the effectiveness of teaching and the overall quality of education.

The last point concerns the specific use of information science tools in the training of architects at the first, second and third levels. The introduction of these tools into architecture has revolutionised perhaps more than in any other sector the work methods not only of the students or of the researchers, but the entire international system of architecture. There is no need here to recall the radical transformation that the spread of computer tools has brought not only to the production methods of design, but also to the fusion of these design methods with the other technical and scientific documents that are an integral part of architectural production. Also, we need not dwell upon the new impetus to geometric, spatial and dynamic exploration that these new tools have exerted in architectural design. All this is well known and is the main reference point of our research. What I wish to point out is that, despite many experimental initiatives at a local, national and international level which are promising but often, if not always, disappointing or at least not capable of being applied on a significant scale, it can be maintained that the teaching and learning of architectural design cannot take place without a direct contact between teacher and student; in the case of architecture, in fact, it cannot take effect except in a relationship of 'master' and 'pupil'. Ludovico Quaroni often reminded all of us that one of architecture's peculiar features was that it could not be taught by means of an entirely scientific method. Intuition, the essential requirement in architecture, if it is not to be purely artistic expression, can undoubtedly avail itself of a detailed scientific knowledge of a specific design problem, but it cannot ripen except through a close direct relationship that is colloquial, dialectical, exemplary and even contentious, with current architectural thought, with a working architect who has been chosen, for his institutional role or for some transitory cultural affinity, as the master of design. Obviously we are not thinking of either the renaissance 'artist's workshop' or the anonymous medieval schools, although they should be given some reconsideration, in our intimately internationalised, and thus in some ways medievalised, modern world, where the great collective organisations of architectural production have such power. However, the ripening of architectural intuition cannot be achieved through a lengthy, or what is worse, a totally exclusive series of instruments and artifices; we must convince ourselves that it involves a transmission of culture that has aspects that *cannot be entirely rationally analysed or transmitted* – once upon a time one would have said 'ineffable' in the original sense of the term.

Thus our research, even despite its apparent fragmentary appearance, firmly believes in the idea that information science tools and the oNLine System should be utilized in innumerable ways in the various independent stages of an architect's learning itinerary, but that they can never totally replace the maieutic aspect of master-pupil relations, even if the masters, due to the extraordinary capacities of computer science, can be themselves multiplied, since, even though distant in space, they can be visibly and audibly next to us in a shared environment, even interacting with our own designs. We ourselves are spectators with other students gathered from all over the world to share together the most precious and unique moments in our and their educational growth. Research into the most effective way of realising this 'Augmented Reality' as the Americans call it, is our most ambitious objective, along with a parallel investigation into all the other possible stages of teaching in which information science technologies can be used as a normal and potent tool for the training of an architect.

Lucio Valerio Barbera

E-LEARNING FOR ARCHITECTURE

A didactic approach for beginners

Distance learning has become a matter of strategic importance in education; demographically and economically decisive, and politically correct, it is an issue that the international university community has for some time felt the need to deal with.

It is a relatively new approach, since it is continuously evolving and being updated, and can be described as a function of two variables: that of technological progress and development which rapidly transforms a new discovery into a commercial product, making all others redundant in the space of a few months, and secondly, the variable of the desiderata of a society craving for resources, to be consumed impersonally like fast food.

The initial enthusiasm for distance education, fostered and promoted over the last twenty years by European policies in line with worldwide tendencies, has faded or rather undergone some second thoughts and doubts in the first years of the twenty-first century, after about a decade of experimentation, promotion and programmes and the setting up of a large number of international networks and collaborations.

The number of organisations engaged in e-learning today is impressive: *European Distance E-learning Network, IEEE Education Society, EL-European Institute for E-Learning, European Learning Industry Group, Journal of Online Education, International Journal of Emerging Technologies in Learning*, etc. The list can be continued at length with much repetition of key terms and contents. Influential leaders from some of these organisations quite openly admit to the 'mass approach' behind these systems, and maintain that the use of distance learning has more to do with educating the maximum number of people than with raising educational standards[1].

Rem Koolhas, the architect who won the Prietzke prize in 2000 and who is fascinated by the generic spaces – airports and fast food outlets – of the generic city, said something similar in recent interviews: *"what is good in the world is something that does not interest me"*, indirectly giving a reason why e-learning, especially in its extensive commercial versions, is the correct response to a demand for mass education.

Like the network of global companies, distance education is an enterprise active 24/7. It is no wonder that the students who up to now have opted for this kind of education belong to the category of working students (often adults). However, the 'distance' option is beginning to attract younger students, mainly because it gives them more free time and also because in many countries university attendance is too expensive. In Italy the first disciplines to invest in distance learning methods were those of medicine and paramedics; Rome Sapienza, in its medical courses, made use of an e-learning platform, *Blackboard*. The users of e-learning software are divided between the defenders of commercial products and those who prefer open source software.

Trying to orient oneself in the universe of more or less commercial distance learning can be complicated, requiring market appraisals more within the field of a professional buyer. After examining a certain number of tools and methods one comes to the conclusion that "effective use of computer science and telematics is not a different way of doing the same thing (teaching); it is doing a different thing"[2].

The problem is understanding the meaning of 'doing a different thing' in our specific discipline, that of architecture, and seeing if there is a possibility of developing tools and methods for training architects using the most up-to-date information technologies.

Before, and apart from, the introduction of e-learning tools, the information revolution over the past twenty years has transformed the profession of architect and has sparked off an intellectual debate that has led many to believe that apart from traditional architecture there exists a 'digital architecture' and that the use of such **tools** is not only the latest evolutionary stage of a form of writing (considered to be the greatest revolution in our civilisation), but is a process that can engender new **methods** of designing space.

---

[1] See Bray, H., Maeroff, G., R., Massy, W. Zemsky, R., (2007, January). E-learning: successes and failures. *Chronicle of Higher Education*, Vol. 53.

[2] See Mark C. Taylor, *The Moment of Complexity*, Codice Edizioni, Torino 2005.

There has been scholarly debate for some time now on whether distance learning can be considered as potential way of creating a new form of cultural product, covering a vast range of products from book publishing to theatre performances. Most recent surveys reveal that 60% of universities in the world use e-learning in combination with traditional teaching, whereas a much smaller percentage offer courses entirely conducted on-line. In Italy, investments by universities in e-learning are on the increase, while in Britain and especially in America there has been a decrease, due also to the fact that the largest investments were made ten years ago. Other surveys show that students tend to use and learn graphic software to independently create their own web sites and e-portfolios. It would appear, therefore, more useful to invest in the possibility that the added value of Open and Distance Education – which has been shown not to be self-sufficient as a teaching system – corresponds to its undeniable potential to create and manage internet communities in the most flexible and creative way possible, and yet encourage a 'mixed' model, that of blended learning.

In order to investigate the relationship between informatics tools and the methods and results of teaching, the research programme PRIN 2006 was set up: 'Research and experimentation of new information models and technologies for distance teaching of architects', of which a summary is given in this paper.

Organisation of the research

The research team is based on national research groups who had already taken part, in 2000, in the WINDS project (Web based INtelligent Design tutoring System) sponsored by the *eEurope* plan of the European Commission. Despite its limitations, acknowledged by many among its authors and participants, WINDS can be seen as an indispensible stage in the assessment of e-learning, without which it would have been impossible to make the corrections, find the alternatives and effect the developments in this new PRIN 2006 project.

The work carried out by almost all the Research Units can be divided into two major groupings: one dealing with the survey of the tools and applications, and the other on the investigation of the methods and didactics for architecture.

The survey of the tools and applications was carried out principally by:
- Rosalba Belibani and Luca Fabbri (Rome Sapienza) who, while organising and setting up an *e-workshop,* carried out a survey on the available e-learning platforms (both commercial and open source) and produced a comprehensive description of the applications provided in their didactic and methodological and evaluative aspects.
- Mario Petrone, (Università degli Studi del Molise), who carried out an analysis of didactic models and technological tools in order not only to choose not only which didactic tools were needed in designing a proper learning itinerary but also the way to which tools were intended to be used.
- Liliana Bazzanella and Luca Caneparo (Politecnico di Torino), who described the work carried out in virtual laboratories for urban simulation, explaining the methods used and their significance for teaching.
- Gianluigi Mondaini, Alberto Giretti, Mario De Grassi and Roberta Ansuini (Università Politecnica delle Marche), who describe the prospects of Cognitive Research for Design and the requirements for e-learning design courses.
- Stefano Panunzi (Università degli Studi del Molise), who provided a detailed chronological record of his researches into tele-contiguity over the past ten years. Apart from the innovations in designing e-learning platforms which will undoubtedly appear on the market, Panunzi's seems to be the most important among the current experiments, above all for the special spatial and temporal conditions it can create.

The survey on methodologies applied to teaching was carried out mainly by:
- Liliana Bazzanella, Luca Caneparo, Gustavo Ambrosini e Michele Bonino (Politecnico di Torino), who experimented with their tools in a vast area of teaching and in distance workshops with two Asian faculties.
- Paolo Desideri and Milena Farina, who placed at our disposal their researches on the city, architecture and design, in particular Paolo Desideri's didactic 'performance' which was video-recorded, dismantled and reassembled in order to construct learning objects, which the research unit of Rome Sapienza used in setting up workshops with the students.
- Anna Irene Del Monaco (Rome Sapienza), who presented a report on the state of the

art in e-learning and the most recent inclinations of experts towards 'blended learning'.

- Lucio Barbera and Anna Irene Del Monaco (Rome Sapienza), who for two years experimented with using the Moodle platform in their courses of design and dissertation planning, and an e- workshop in collaboration with the entire Research Unit of Rome Sapienza and their students.

- Rosalba Belibani and Luca Fabbri (Rome Sapienza), who tested the validity of the Moodle platform in the e-workshop and presented an analysis of the results.
- Rosalba Belibani (Rome Sapienza), who experimented for four years with a design course entirely on-line, implemented with blended learning methods.

Anna Irene Del Monaco

The roots of research

Rosalba Belibani

The research presented in this volume has its roots in a long history dedicated to the development of multimedia for the architecture and its educational and social communication, under the enlightened auspices of Paola Coppola Pignatelli who since 1986 has directed a group research on issues related to ITC, the Dipartimento di Progettazione Architettonica e Urbana, at the Faculty of Architecture of the Università di Roma "La Sapienza", where she established, in 1998, the LaMA_Laboratorio Multimediale di Architettura. The research team came about following an ealier research by Stefano Panunzi and Rosalba Belibani on multimedia and its relationship between architecture and its role in the construction and communication of architectural design. Listed below is a summary of some of the important stages in this long journey of research, full of significant and fruitful moments, and always oriented towards the achievement of objectives demonstrated to be important steps towards future sustainable technologies.

- University Research MURST 40% *"The production of multimedia teaching circuits for Architecture and Urbanism"*, 1991-'93. Within the research two hypertexts were produced entitled "Barcelona: hypertext reading of a city" and "Cities ipervisible: Seville, Barcelona, Lisbona".
- IMARA '93 (Image et Animée Architectural Representation), *Animated Image and Architectural Representation*, Montecarlo 1993.
- The International Conference *"Multimedia for Teaching Architecture"*, Roma, Congress Centre "La Sapienza", 1997.
- Estabhished LaMA_Laboratorio Multimediale di Architettura, Dipartimento di Progettazione Architettonica e Urbana, Università di Roma "La Sapienza", 1998.
- Inter-University Research Communications hypertext architecture on the existential comfort between the Faculty of Architecture and the Faculty of Sociology, national coordinator Prof. Paola Coppola Pignatelli, 1999..
- Production of hypertext on CD-Rom, *Journey in the City of the Third Millennium*, developed at the Multimedia LaMA_Laboratorio Multimediale di Architettura, Dipartimento di Progettazione Architettonica e Urbana, in agreement with the Banca Nazionale del Lavoro, 1999-2000. Hypertext shows an image of a hypothetical city of the future that draws on many buildings and parts of the city built in the last ten years by the most famous architects in Europe, North America, Japan and Oceania. Widely used in education, this multimedia tool has been successfully presented at the Conference MDA2 Architecture & Multimedia, Moebius Award City of Lugano, 7. International Architecture Exhibition of Venice Biennale Less Aesthetics More Ethics.
- International Conference *"MDA2 Architecture & Multimedia"*, Roma, 2000. Presentation of the CD Rom *Journey in the City of the Third Millennium*.
- EU Research WINDS - Web based Intelligent Design Tutoring System. This research developed the potential of multimedia for teaching design and completed online teaching modules for architectural students. The Rome based Research Unit, coordinated by Prof. P. Coppola Pignatelli, worked on *"Archaetipical contents for the project planning for innovative design"*, 2000-'03.
- Exhibition *"local / global"*, the video review of Architecture and Lama Video Library, Roma, 2002.
- Exhibition *"5 Departments of Architecture at the Venice Biennale"*, Venezia Arsenale Le Tese, 2002.
- Dvd video presentation *"From architecture to the architecture of the connections of the fence. From the architecture to the architecture of the boundaries of the links"*, International Conference *Enclosures which messages architectural building envelopes as architecture's messages*, Napoli, 2003.

The results of Research PRIN 2006 presented in this volume, represent the latest segment of almost twenty years of national and international research on the subject and demonstrate a significant phase of shared research and development of new architectural technolgies.

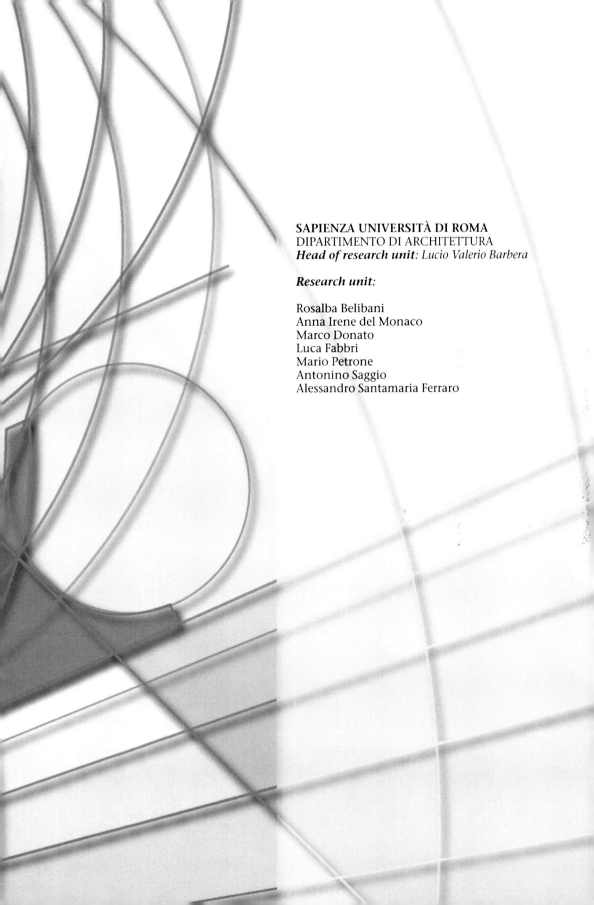

SAPIENZA UNIVERSITÀ DI ROMA
DIPARTIMENTO DI ARCHITETTURA
Head of research unit: Lucio Valerio Barbera

Research unit:

Rosalba Belibani
Anna Irene del Monaco
Marco Donato
Luca Fabbri
Mario Petrone
Antonino Saggio
Alessandro Santamaria Ferraro

E-learning for architecture on web platforms: e-workshops

Rosalba Belibani
Luca Fabbri

1. E-LEARNING PLATFORMS AS DIDACTIC TOOLS

In the 1990's, at the same time as a European-level awareness of *lifelong learning* was being created (cf. the Lifelong Learning Programme 2007-2013), various university laboratories innovative experiments into on-line teaching. This was for the most part for personal translation undertakings and isolated experiments to apply and synthesise the new ICT (Information and Communication Technologies) into teaching and training systems, without the use of any complex interface platforms. In trying to move universities away from *dual mode* (frontal teaching with some distance learning) to *mixed mode* systems (both modes in parallel), platforms (interface structures) were needed where more courses could be run, initially only from an administrative standpoint. Recently, as a further step in the process of transforming universities into virtual models (U-Virtual, universities which provide virtual courses by means of specific software), performative environments were created on the Web for collaborative learning and the formation of inter-disciplinary knowledges (as a progressive process for problem solving) and the acquisition of expertise.

This process of transformation has led to the creation of platforms that can be used for e-learning (both commercial and non-commercial) which are increasingly available and used on the internet. Some are little known, since they are oriented towards research or addressed to small groups of users, while others are highly visible, with huge numbers of parallel visits daily. Many of these are used by important bodies whose primary purpose is not teaching but who turn to e-learning for the in-house training of specialised personnel. The presence of several platforms should be seen not as a hindrance but rather as an opportunity, since it offers both teachers and students a choice of tools of high quality that compete with one another thus encouraging a high standard of performance and the pursuit of excellence.

1.1 A survey of the principal e-learning platforms

We here briefly describe the features of some of the more important platforms examined and how they can be implemented for teaching purposes, which is the aim of our research.

Blackboard
Commercial web site: *http://www.blackboard.com*
This platform is a commercial software package which

thanks to its multi-layered architecture is aimed at universities and other institutions, both large and small, whose principal function is educational. With its modular structure, it enables the user to improve and personalise the functions offered by combining them with software packages called building blocks, which includes data bases and other applications. The flexibility of this software means that the user environment, the graphic interface, profiles and privileges of each user can be *customised*. Blackboard possesses advanced tools for evaluation, on-line test management, results and didactic activities of the student. The technical support supplied directly by the software producer guarantees maintenance and assistance facilities at a 'mission critical' level. The platform is used in various Italian faculties in *blended* form for teaching, for the sharing of didactic materials, for the collaboration between users (teachers and students) and the assessment of students' performance. The educational offices of the Central Administration of Sapienza Università di Roma use the platform for the training of technical and administrative staff and student assistants. The Blackboard package enables the user to file as well as import/export contents according to current standards. The system possesses a high level of scalability which enables it to handle from a few dozen to hundreds of thousands of users while maintaining high performance levels and continuous availability of access. The maximum number of courses, of recordable users and suppliable content depends on the hardware characteristics of the server. The platform includes collaboration tools such as virtual classrooms, chat, etc. Its open, modular structure means that it can be functionally augmented with other software packages. Training courses and free seminars of one or two days are held annually on request of the faculty or other interested institution.

Moodle
Web site: *http://moodle.org/*

Sapienza Università di Roma web site: *http://e-learning.uniroma1.it*

The E-learning Moodle software platform is an open source software package, freely downloadable from *http://download.moodle.org/*, initially created by Martin Dougiamas in 1999. The man behind this open source project, which is now used by tens of thousands all over the world, has a post graduate degree in Computer Science and Education and a PhD whose thesis subject was "The use of Open Source software to support a social constructionist epistemology of teaching and learning within internet-based communities of reflective inquiry". The philosophy behind the Moodle project is the *theory of collaborative learning*, which has by now been installed in every country and in every language of the world.

The open source[1] platform, freely available on the internet, which can be implemented cost-free without any start up licence fee or user's fee, offers high-quality solutions that have been developed and tested with the help of prestigious universities all over the world. Moodle was chosen as an e-learning open source platform for Rome Sapienza, following stud-

E-LEARNING FOR ARCHITECTURE

ies carried out by CITICoRD, for its valid features of completeness, reliability and user-friendliness. The platform was adopted by many other Italian and foreign universities besides Rome, including the University of Eastern Piedmont and the universities of Cagliari, Bari, Genoa, Modena and Reggio, Padua, Florence, Perugia, Turin, Sannio, Sassari, Siena, Urbino and Trieste. Abroad, Moodle is the official platform of the Open University in the UK and Athabasca University in Canada.

Moodle conforms to all the major international standards of e-learning, including AICC and ADL SCORM and can import data from standard systems and from all the more important existing e-learning systems. It can import student lists in LDAP format and entire quiz databases prepared in Blackboard or WebCT. It was developed in accordance with the requirements of accessibility of Section 508 and of the XHTML 1.0 Transitional standard published by W3C, and was adapted to the accessibility requirements of the Stanca Law (GU 9/1/2004, n° 4). The system has a high scalability and can cater to from a few dozen to hundreds of thousands of users while maintaining high performance levels and continuous availability of access. Moodle provides synchronous communication, thanks to Wimba software. It efficiently integrates and automatically activates the personal identifiers of the most important and widespread messaging software, audio- and video-conferencing (messenger, ICQ, Skype, Yahoo) into the profile of every participant.

NetLearning

This platform is a commercial software system created for a pilot inter-university Master project funded by the MIUR, involving 11 Faculties of Medicine and Surgery in Italy. Technically it consists of a VPN-IP (INTRANET) between the universities; its frame of reference is a complete integrated e-learning platform that guarantees the provision of educational activities, both synchronous and asynchronous, on a hybrid terrestrial-satellite communications platform. NetLearning is a system for managing on-line teaching and learning, with both synchronous and asynchronous distribution, and with a high level of scalability, modularity, integration and personalisation. The platform uses innovative structural and methodological technologies for distance learning. Apart from transmitting live or recorded events to a wide public, it gives users a series of tools providing a high level of interactivity between participants. The access portal to the e-learning facilities allows the educational material on offer to be managed synchronously, by means of the concept of virtual classrooms (NetLearning Classroom) and asynchronously by using NetLearning LCMS.

The logic architecture of the system includes: the portal as access point to the platform for all users and for the uploading of content, the virtual classroom system, the LCMS for using the didactic content asynchronously and the author system for creating and managing backup teaching material. The platform conforms to standards and reference protocols for security (https, Single Sign On, LDAP) and for e-learning (SCORM, IMS, AICC, IMS QTI), technologies enabling integrability, inter-operability and cooperation applications like

XML and Web Services e technologies enabling forms of business like *e-commerce, e-Learning, Service Provider.*

[from: P. Renzi, S. Basili, R. Belibani, A. Di Ciaccio, G. Luciani, C. Napoleoni, V. Papaspyropoulos, E. Valentini, *Assessment of the technology and creation of guidelines for its use. Assessment of minimum requirements and preparation of guidelines for distance learning quality*, for: Survey on the use of the Web in Teaching, University Commission on Teaching Innovations Ruggero Matteucci (President of the Commission) and Andrea Lenzi (Coordinator of the working Group of Faculty e-learning delegates) November 2007].

ADA (Digital Learning Environment)
Web site: *http://ada.lynxlab.com*

ADA is an open source e-learning system designed and developed by Lynx which supplies a well-structured series of facilities that can manage and combine *on or off-line multimedia courses, didactic support via internet,* and access to *shared resources* with information-flow management. It is an entirely web-based *multimedia and multi-mode system* which originated in meetings between teachers, students and parents of altrascuola.it and Lynx, a company designing and creating teaching software; the system is distributed in its entirety under GPL licence, with its first version appearing in 2001; the latest version, 1.8, is due to appear in September 2009.

ADA was designed in such a way as to highlight the real needs of its users in all their possible roles: as students, tutors, authors and administrators. It is based on a participatory learning model heavily weighted towards continuous learning. This model, called '*spiral*' sees on-line education as a growth opportunity for both individuals and organisations, which can be fulfilled through a continuous *interactive exchange between the knowledge of all participants.* An analysis of pre-existing e-learning systems and the use of the spiral model were the basis of the planning and development stage, where certain essential points were noted regarding technical information aspects and didactic requirements, in order to obtain the best educational results.

The *structure of an ADA course* comprises *minimal units* (nodes) connected by links and with external multi-medial resources. This changes the courses into *extensive knowledge networks* which *teachers* can organise using *lesson generator* modules, where the *students* can browse and add to their knowledge. The ADA courses consist of *subsets of nodes, links and resources* which are not determined once and for all by the author, but are constantly updated by the activities and by the students during the time span of the course. The most impressive feature of the *ADA Lessons Generator* is its *graphic interface* which lets the author see both parallel (nodes at the same level) and hierarchical (groups of nodes) relationships. ADA includes a form of *discussion forum* which is an integral part of the course, where the discussion threads are the actual nodes of the course; it is also very effective in evaluation and self-assessment and allows for an *on-going management of evaluation* through the mechanism of *level filters* and *dynamic indices.*

ADA is written entirely in a single scripting language from the server side PHP and is a multi-layered package, where Logic/Interface/Database are clearly distinguished. The system is accessible with no limitations on the machine, operating system, or connection speed (it is based on DataBase SQL) and is extremely versatile in that it allows the user to modify all the features of the interface.

Saba Learning Enterprise
Web Site: *http://www.saba.com*

Saba offers high-profile commercial e-learning platforms which are extremely prominent on the world market thanks to their ability to be adapted to complex and diverse circumstances. Saba LMS provides unique functions for the integrated management of educational processes, enabling the learning processes, performance assessment, production and allocation of content to be automated and resources to be optimised with a view to promoting and cultivating intellectual capital within different companies. The platform is based on an open architecture, created on Java and XML standards, which can be integrated with ERP, CRM and HR systems and can be entirely handled in remote by clients on the Web. The architecture of Saba follows modular design criteria that guarantee ease of access, updating and modification of system components, with both ordinary and extraordinary maintenance costs kept to a minimum.

With *Saba Publisher* and *Saba Content*, didactic resources of different kinds and formats can be composed for the creation of courses and learning itineraries that are mixed and can be personalised to learners' needs. *Saba LMS* promotes the development of specific skills connected to precise business objectives by means of *Saba Performance*, which can identify crucial educational itineraries.

With this platform, various kinds of multi-medial materials and content can be distributed, from simple .pdf to learning objects in scorm format, and the single didactic units can be built into modules, which can be administered and allocated independently or organised into ad hoc learning itineraries, personalised to individual needs. From the teacher's point of view, Saba has been designed to enable and support mixed learning processes, *Blended Learning*, where distance learning (synchronous on-line, virtual classrooms, videoconferencing, etc.) alternates with asynchronous learning (films and pre-recorded lessons).

Using Saba, the results and performances of the courses can be monitored effectively through an extremely detailed and complete *tracing* system, which allows teachers to obtain information on the use of the system at both individual student and class level. Performance statistics (display times on the entire content or on single teaching units, percentage of visual presentation, and so on) can be compiled, and naturally data on any evaluation tests present (attempts made, percentage of correct answers, statistics on individual items, etc.). Here we have a wide-ranging, well-constructed monitoring system, which can become a feedback tool for the teacher and also an indispensible framework for evidence of the learning itinerary that has been followed, and where necessary, for its documentary authentication.

2.a-b
Images from the telecontiguity session between the Research Units of Rome and Termoli.

Saba is capable of structuring an enormous number of types of user, differentiating them by environment (internal users, universities, firms, etc.) or by role (learners, teachers, tutors, etc.) and can assign to each one certain privileges of visualisation, of courses, of uses or even of modifying contents; contents are organised in a catalogue and each subscriber has their own file with all personal details and their overall educational profile.

1.2 The choice of MOODLE as reference platform

Choosing one of the various e-learning platforms that we have described above is the decisive preliminary step towards setting up an e-learning process. The principal aim after all of our research is to present and try out a global teaching method for e-learning in Architecture. The chosen platform must therefore be suitable for the teaching of architecture courses and take into account the user base and the scalability of the system, as well as have an infrastructure capable of guaranteeing to every user a comprehensible synchronous access to the courses offered by the server.

The Saba, Blackboard and Moodle platforms, which are probably the most well-known and used worldwide, satisfy our requirements perfectly; they present numerous similarities between themselves and are all versatile in the synchronous aspects of e-learning. However, our choice has to be Moodle, since it is unique in its *open source* platform features. Among the applications implementable on the platform, we were very interested in the Wimba package, which can collect and use simultaneously communication and interactive features such as *forums, chat, blogs* and *wiki*, integrating them with advanced sharing systems such as virtual classrooms, *desktop sharing* and *application sharing*, video-communication via web cam (one-to-one or one-to-group), and the possibility of filing the chronology of events in a repository. Wimba provides those activities that are useful for e-learning where the common denominator is the simplification, from the teacher's standpoint, of the translation (*scorm*) of certain traditional applications and the activation, for everyone, of a classroom and a shared, interactive, contiguous space/desktop. Experiments were made with the use of the Moodle platform, after the survey, as a tool integrated into traditional didactic activities for two consecutive academic years, within various courses of architecture.

2. THE CREATION OF AN E-LEARNING COURSE: THE EXPERIENCE OF A WORKSHOP ON THE MOODLE PLATFORM

2.1 Creation of a prototype e-learning course.

It should be made clear once and for all that translating a course structured in a traditional way into a web course does not mean that one has created a real e-learning course. If one does not make full use, even as an experiment, of the technologies offered by the web and platforms for new concepts of teaching and new appliances for them, then one is merely making a translation without any idea of what one is talking about. The various tools of information science that have been introduced into traditional teaching have brought considerable changes in communication and evaluation, but it is definitively more important to understand how much the new technologies in e-learning can be beneficial to teaching and learning and how they can lead to substantial reciprocal involvement. The potential of web 1 and web 2 can free the teacher from well-established didactic procedures but can also at the same time liberate the student by offering him or her a more personal, detailed, collaborative and transversal learning method.

When creating an e-learning course, the first questions to ask are the following: What type of course do we want to create? What are the aims of the course? What are the most suitable tools to use? How do we want our students to work? What kind if environment do we want them to work in?

To each of these questions there corresponds a choice of optional information tools and a construction protocol which follows certain general methodological rules, and which must necessarily be used in connection with other communicative strategies. Each of the personalities involved, teacher, student, tutor, administrator, future didactic translator, has his own idea of the opportunities on offer, and of the objectives and results of the enterprise. Last but not least, the academic discipline, the subject, has a fundamental role to play in how the course is envisaged, in the quality of its content, its aesthetic features and its specific didactic rules.

2.2 Translation of the didactic content: 'The origins of the contemporary'. Technical problems, solutions and teaching implications

The most interesting aspect from a teaching point of view, as often happens in the construction of an e-learning module, was the translation of research topics, previously developed by the RU of Università degli Studi Roma Tre, into an on-line teaching form. We organised the material into a lavishly indexed text, with lists of architects and their works, a glossary of materials and a bibliography. To better interpret the data we created an initial grid which set out the relationships in parallel between aspects of the urban, technological, residential and figurative culture in the modern era and in the contemporary age. This matrix suggested to us that the access to the data should not be structured sequentially, but by topic and image-linked.

Our aim, therefore, within the technical limits of the platform interface, was to design a structure that was still indexed but which implied an access that was not only sequential but linear or parallel, on demand. Since the course had to be of necessity organised according to paradigms of files, actions, diagrams and specifications, we wanted all of this to represent in its completeness and originality, the subject of the course, its field of discipline and characterised by its didactic and technological inter-disciplinary nature. For this purpose we trans-

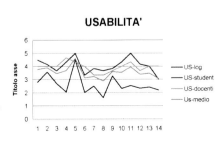

3.
Graphs of Learning and Usability drawn up following the analysis of the data deriving from the questionnaires and the logs.

4.
Graph of Frequency of Access, drawn up after the analysis of the logs to estimate the visits and lengths of stay of the students.

formed the didactic grid into an interactive panoramic diagram with direct links to chapters and key topics, and thus to video files, .doc files and on-line glossaries.

Once the basic formal translation of the course contents had been organised, we went on to the practical creation of the e-learning course on the Moodle platform. In building the didactic structure for the dedicated workshop, we took into account the considerations, expressed in the second stage of the activities of the first year, on the kinds of systems to adopt, which had been tried out individually, and in the final experiment suitably revised. The aims of the experiments were:

- Construction of a 'real' lesson ad hoc, organised efficiently according to different communication modes (audio/video or interactive files, etc.).
- Creation of easily accessible audio/video clips. Audio-only files were prepared, downloadable on smart phone or ipod, to speed up the performance of the lesson and make it more versatile.
- Links to other tools and contents present on the net (google earth, live maps, youtube, etc.) for parallel navigation and in order to manage the traditional basic activities transferred into digital acts on the web
- Entering new contents into the partially pre-established glossaries on the part of the student, who while following the course can embellish it with information of their own;
- Transmission of live or recorded educational events to a public distributed over the territory;
- The use of another series of tools to ensure a high level of interaction between the participants;
- Capture screen of recordings for repository purposes.

A set of rapid iconographic navigation-dedicated menus was created during the construction of the course. For example, in the *References* block we placed all the textual and iconographic glossaries belonging to the course, such as: *The architects, The works, Figurative culture, Materials, Technologies, Enterprises*. We had created a large number of cards for every topic area which formed a database that could be easily implemented and integrated by both teachers and students, where each new item was automatically linked to the course contents. This scope for interaction and constant updating of the database is one of the more interesting aspects of e-learning since it both actively engages the learner and is able to construct a didactic cultural repository for the course.

In the resources blocks, also, a classification of web resources freely available on the net was added to Tools and facilities for teaching. These technological inputs, organised in the form of glossaries, containing a brief description and the relative URL, were made available to both teachers and students. In identifying and grouping these tools and facilities we took account of the different stages of the process of collaboration: *sharing – participating – commenting – collaborating – creating – spreading – classifying – assembling – re-elaborating – grouping – underwriting – decentralising – distributing – finding and being found*. Specific tools named after common actions correspond to these stages.

5.
Image of the home page of the e-Workshop 'The Origins of the Contemporary' as seen on iPhone.

3. Analysis of results: the evaluation tool

Within the e-learning platform complex forms of evaluation on the quality of the course can be carried out through the assessment of the actors involved (teachers, students, translators, tutors, etc.) and the evaluation of the results achieved by the students during the course with respect to the objectives of the course itself. These assessments, increasingly required by university managements, are, in the e-learning mode, immediate and real. The model can evaluate through feedback the correct functioning of the platform and its usability in terms of efficiency.

Evaluating the Workshop

As the intensive thematic workshop was created as a resource, we prepared a protocol for the control evaluation of the experimental stage, in collaboration with the UDR of Ancona. At first, the evaluation of results called for the comparison of methods; or rather, our initial intention was to check the efficiency of the 'e-learning method' by comparing it with the traditional method of teaching. This classic manner of verification was soon shown to be outdated when it became obvious that the set up of the translation of the teaching content already demonstrated particular qualities, enriched as it was by various media and intensified vertically and horizontally by means of *links* and *wikis*. It was immediately obvious that the entire structure could not be directly transmitted with traditionally taught lessons and the objectives that were being developed would be very difficult to achieve in a course taught in the traditional way. We therefore directed our experimentation towards a single goal, that of functioning internally by means of analyses and evaluation of the learning processes only within the 'e-learning group'.

To this end we devised a protocol which used three types of tool:

- Evaluation of the *learning* by assessing the students' performance. A brief pre-questionnaire was prepared (to be answered by the students on the platform, before the start of the workshop – see Appendix A) to check the student's starting level, and an evaluation of performance card (for the teacher – see Appendix B). The results obtained were then compared statistically.
- Evaluation of the tool used by the students in the e-learning group. The students were asked to compile a post-questionnaire on the Likert scale, to measure how the approach suggested by the end-users had been perceived (see Appendix C).
- Evaluation of the effective system-user interaction by means of the system logs (see Appendix D).

For the 'e-learning group' learning of the contents took place by participating exclusively in the workshop through the Moodle platform, where the 'workshop package' entitled 'The origins of the Contemporary' had been installed. At the end of the workshop the students were asked to produce a report and/or a presentation that described the contents they had learned, on which the teachers had made their evaluation.

6.
Image of the home page of the e-Workshop 'The Origins of the Contemporary' as seen on iPhone.

The results obtained were statistically correlated as shown in the graphs, as regards the following evaluation objectives:
- *learning* understood in terms of:
  - level of learning
  - lacquisition of a structure of conceptual knowledge
  - lability to associate the contents
- lthe *practical aspects* of the tool (conformity to objective: improving learning)
  - the *usability – use effectiveness* of the tool (how much the student had used the tool compared with its predicted potential)

The graphs for further interpretation are shown below.

As far as regards the evaluation of the effective system-user interaction and the possibility of tracing the frequency of visits and method of navigation of each individual student participating in the workshop, the *logs* tool was found to be extremely useful. We were particularly interested in two aspects that we regarded as especially important and which can be analysed separately.

The first aspect was the simple yet indicative record of the numbers and distribution of individual accesses. This provided useful information on how each student uses his or her study time. From the relevant graph there clearly emerges (along with a reduction in deviations and exceptions) an ever-increasing generalised frequency of visits. This tendency reaches a peak at around 2/3 of the entire time spent, and then drops slightly until a further intense frequency towards the end point (the closing of the workshop and handing in of work done).

Further information can be gained by analysing the distribution of accesses within the span of a single day, and by examining the relation between the number of visits and their duration. Here the data shows a marked dissimilarity in approach. While some students opt for a few yet consistent daily 'session', others prefer more numerous but shorter visits. We must however always remember that a considerable part of the student's activities cannot be followed, since they do not take place on-line.

The second aspect concerns the 'route' followed by the student while consulting the didactic materials. Here a brief explanation is needed. When preparing these materials, we opted for solutions that were not excessive in the use of learning objects. According to the level of granular structure (especially when the pre-packaging of these self-consistent units becomes excessive), these objects run the risk of nullifying any qualities of collaboration and interaction that an e-learning course should possess. By choosing to give precedence to the parcelling out of independent resources rather than to their standardisation, we had the positive advantage of increasing our ability to trace the path taken by a student while avoiding any excessive conditions in the use of the materials. We were able to observe that, in the majority of cases, when students first accessed the on-line course, they explored the contents in a way that was anything but ordered and sequential. The student initially surveyed the resources and tools available by browsing all over, jumping forwards and changing direction. Only afterwards did he or she follow a logical and ordered

7.
Frames of the videos integrated into the text of the lesson, visible in the e-Workshop 'The Origins of the Contemporary' on the Moodle platform.

path. This is one particular way in which an e-learning course differs from a traditional course, where the learning times are much more regulated and regimented; classes take place at pre-determined hours and the receiving of information happens at speeds and in sequences that are the same for everyone. Obviously it is perfectly possible to organise an on-line course according to a rigid teaching calendar. One could decide to make the material available one piece at a time, determine deadlines and handing-in times, and control timescales and delays. In fact, finding the most appropriate choices at a formal level for establishing times for study is in itself an interesting point for reflection.

We would like to also point out the possibilities offered by the logs, when it comes to examining the effective level of exchanges and reciprocal collaboration between students. The installation of tools that promote collective contributions, mutual assistance and participation in the improvement of contents was in fact carefully planned when we constructed the on-line workshop. The use of glossaries, for example, was very useful in this regard. They were divided into various topics and provided with a standard card with images and text; they were designed, however, in such a way that the students, when prompted, could combine them, comment on them, or add new contents or items to them, and in this way become involved in a process of participation and collaboration. By analysing the logs we were able to monitor when and how this activity took place.

4. DIDACTIC ASPECTS AND THEIR TRANSPOSITION INTO E-LEARNING: GUIDELINES

4.1 Interaction and communication tools: synchronous and asynchronous methods

Obviously, in an e-learning project the established objectives must be given the utmost attention and as far as *teaching methods* are concerned, due consideration should be paid to the weighting (and aspects) of the *informative* and *collaborative* stages. In the specific case of the teaching of Architecture, for instance, the particular nature of the type of study involves a need for the teacher to evaluate the evolution of the students' project work (reviews). Not only the more traditional type of communal lesson where the teacher explains, demonstrates and illustrates, and the students observe, listen and eventually intervene (an informative event); but also essential sessions of teacher-student meetings on the work produced (a collaborative event). This latter activity, when the teacher comments, corrects and provides precise indications, intervening directly in the graphic designs produced by the student, can take place, in part, asynchronously: the student's work can be subjected to the teacher's review by sending it by e-mail, in other words, without any recourse to particularly advanced tools. This naturally involves a greater degree of freedom in organising individual timetables (there is no need to be tied to a specific time by an on-line appointment); however, the review process is often less effective and more difficult to carry out.

On the other hand, the synchronous method, following a maieutic form of teaching, guarantees a much higher level of interaction, thanks to the large number of computer tools now available.

A survey revealed an increasingly wide range of applications designed to implement and improve these types of communication, often devised as *freeware* and *open source* software. As well as the more well known and used tools on the net (such as, for example, *audio and textual chat*) there were more advanced tools available, from *virtual classrooms* to *videoconferencing*, from *desktop sharing* to *application sharing*.

Our research experiments with the *Wimba Collaboration Suite*, recently installed within the Moodle platform at Rome Sapienza, were effective here. This suite possesses a high degree of interactivity at both single-single and single-group levels. The *live classroom* is also extremely useful, where numbers of users can communicate both in video and audio and participate either publically or privately in general interactions.

Another important aspect from the teaching standpoint is that entire sessions with the chronology of their events can be recorded and filed for future reference and can be sent to a thematic teaching repository. Thanks to additional plug-ins, one can also easily create multimedia files in word (with both audio and video) which conform to the SCORM standard (*Shareable Content Object Reference Model*), a virtual model which, using various technical specifications within it, is capable of exchanging digital contents independently of the platform. The result is a single compressed file which is perfectly sustainable by Moodle. Taking into account the specific nature of the teaching of Architecture, the possibilities offered by desktop sharing and application sharing (both also integrated into Wimba) are extensive. These are interaction setups in which the two participants in a session can see the contents of each other's computer and also, more importantly, have remote control of the desktop and applications. The advantages are undeniable: the more important files are   managed locally while the information found on the net, regarding for the most part control, are of lesser importance. It thus becomes possible for the teacher to intervene directly on files that are extremely content-heavy and which a student would find difficult to send or present (imagine for example an on-line review on a file such as CAD).

We also made experiments with these tools on computers with different operating systems (MAC/PC) without coming across any significant problem. In some cases we found that the presence of firewalls could cause difficulties and interfere with these kinds of applications. We also noted that the speed of interaction was not always satisfactory.

Tele-contiguity

To our survey and use of communication tools we can add the parallel and complementary experiments carried out of a novel apparatus for distance communication: the *Tele-contiguity Augmented Desk* interface designed and created by the Research Unit at the Università degli Studi del Molise. The unique nature of this tool undoubtedly gives it enormous potential in a synchronous interaction environment. In a similar way to videoconferencing, a collection of technological devices can recreate an environment where the participants enter into dialogues and converse while sharing the same virtual space (as if *de visu*). The system also has another important feature: the perfect coincidence of the contact frames of the participants facing each other. People and objects are targeted and spatially synchronised, giving a realistic sensation of closeness to their reciprocal interaction. Our own Research unit possesses the apparatus for implementing this system and has collaborated in its testing in different contexts. We are convinced that this direction of research will result in further interesting developments thanks to the productive convergence of the use of new technologies and the merits of certain kinds of traditional communication.

4.2 Didactic materials, learning resources, utilisation devices

To achieve a more well-structured form of teaching we obviously need to take into consideration the repertory of didactic materials and the learning resources that these new technologies can provide. However, we do not believe that this means abandoning altogether more traditional learning components. Technological innovations, because of their capacity for further development, are often employed as a replacement for other systems. The possibilities offered, the new horizons that they open up have to be investigated thoroughly and in detail, and at the same time we have to find out when to intervene in an alternative way, when in a complementary fashion. We also have to adopt a clear-cut approach that avoids forcing the issue and that can maintain a good balance. If it is true that the didactic content should be organised and presented to the student by following methods that are appropriate to the means of communication used, it is also true that the choice of method used must correspond to the content to be transmitted.

Very frequently we find cases where the creation of an on-line course originates in the transfer onto the net of a series of traditional lessons. This system is too often reduced to a simple collection of text documents that the student can access on a given site. The increasing spread of e-learning courses is thus not always accompanied by the kind of re-thinking needed to achieve a satisfactory level of re-structuring. All this can be easily observed by consulting the vast offer of on-line teaching to be found on the net.

Even if based around traditional forms, an e-learning course should instead be subjected to the process of 'translation' that can endow it with an *additional value* which the new system in use can provide. This is especially true in the case of forms of teaching which were at their outset designed to be used on the net. At the same time we should remember that in certain cases it is meaningless to 'force' the use of forms of communication which, even if they are technologically advanced, are inevitably totally inappropriate for the didactic content they are called upon to transmit.

Video
For example, video can be used 'naturally' to replace simple slides containing text. As we have observed during our experiments, the use of brief video clips showing the teacher as

he or she introduces and illustrates the various topics of the course in short extracts, is already an effective and incisive aid, since it preserves the tone of voice, timing, facial expressions and gestures of the teacher presenting the lessons.

In any case, video as a teaching aid is extremely valuable. Because of its particular nature, it can transmit messages that are difficult to communicate in any other way. This is especially true in the teaching of architecture, where three-dimensional space, at different scales, is a key element that can only be described effectively through the use of film. This is today even more pertinent if we take into account new technological developments in the field of *reception and communication devices*. In addition to the traditional desk computer and portables such as desktop and notebook, a large amount of new equipment has arrived with which users can consult or surf the net, from netbooks to iPods, and *web mobiles* like iPhone and Blackberry, etc.

Here we can see that we need to add another level to any description of the path taken by a basic didactic component to its end user. If previously it was important to define a suitable relationship between content and method (from a simple text file to an audio or video file, to a more advanced multimedia element) now we have to take into account that the method chosen could be subjected to subsequent modifications because of the *means of reception or consultation* that has been selected (a video downloaded on an iPod will have different features that are a result of the size and scale limits involved, as will also be the case with a website which is navigated using web mobile).

Podcasting

Each of the tools mentioned above present obvious potential advantages and limitations. In the case of podcasting (not necessarily confined to the use of an iPod), by means of a *client programme*, one can put onto the web a series of contents, usually audio-video, a *podcast*, which can be automatically downloaded. This type of resource, which is created in different kinds of compressed formats, is *nomadic* and usable off-line (asynchronously). When the link is made, thanks to the RSS feed technology, new editions of the contents available are automatically signposted. Some educational establishments are still puzzled by these types of technology and show resistance to their adoption, while other prestigious universities (especially in the US and Australia) are using podcasting to distribute all sorts of contents, such as programmes, videoconferences, lecture notes and other materials for the students. To our mind this is podcasting's strongpoint: students are able to receive various kinds of didactic material remotely, and can update their progress continuously thanks to the continual signposting and synchronisation of the contents on offer; all of which, we should point out, does not depend in any way on the system being used.

This last point is quite important. If it is true that the system can be applied to a large number of resources (practically every kind of transmissible file, from simple text documents to advanced multimedia files, from audio-video files to programmes and applications) it is also the case that the use of tools like iPod, as a means of consultation, is somewhat limiting. Apart from the audio/video formats, they are not presently capable of supporting other kinds of formats that allow for a higher level of interactivity. A minimum level of interaction is guaranteed by the use of the tool itself, but navigation inside the individual files takes place for the most part sequentially (compared to other, hypertext, methods, which are in any case available on a computer or on the web). This limitation is partially reduced by the possibility of inserting appropriate markers inside the audio/video files when they are being compiled, which allow the user to move inside the file, passing for example from one chapter to another.

We can definitely state that the use of iPod/e-book can be a possible addition, useful in certain cases (above all in listening) as long as the organisation of the contents that are to be used is carefully thought out beforehand. Here also the observations made previously on the use of video are valid (with an additional limit being the modest size of the screen). A video that can be consulted on an iPod, if it is suitably 'staged' will certainly have a great deal of validity; it should not, however, be reduced to a sterile translation of other kinds of 'presentation'(succession of slides, usually textual, with narrators voice and compulsory time limits).

Web mobile

The same observations can be made in the case of a web mobile (mostly cell phones with web-navigation facility: iPhones, Blackberrys). It is also a small-scale personal portable device which can be used both to consult and to receive. Without a doubt the main advantage of this kind of tool is the opportunity it gives for the user to be moving while accessing the contents; its size and the uses it provides have led to the development of new programming languages, new navigational interfaces, different consultation methods. The most recent language brands, increasingly used for creating web mobile pages, are XHTML and its variants, with which websites can be produced that conform to the standards set down by the W3C (World Wide Web Consortium, an organ that sees to the creation and updating of protocols and specifications for the WWW, with particular regard to accessibility and the development of the net's potential). At the same time, more and more frequently, software is made available for the simplified creation of web mobile pages. Various software houses and major computer manufacturing companies are increasingly involved in this sector, with web applications and guidelines for an improved development of web-based software to be used with these tools. Especially in the USA, the educational world and the business world work hand to hand in this area. Following an agreement between Apple and several major universities such as Stanford, UC Berkeley, MIT and others, on line videos, podcasts and various kinds of didactic material were made available through iTunes U, the sector of iTunes Store dedicated to the universities. Stanford University has gone even further: it recently activated on-line, in the form of a podcast, a special course in iPhone Programming directed at its own information science students and specifically designed for the teaching of applications programming for iPhone and iPod. The course, which was subsequently made available free to everyone in the iTunes U section of the university, in a brief space of time registered a million downloads.

NOTES

[1] *Open source*: software in which the authors enable users to have unrestricted study and also the possibility of modifications and integrations being made by other independent programmers. This kind of extended and often spontaneous collaboration gives the final product a level of complexity and productivity far higher than that which could be obtained by a single working group.

[2] *Log*: a chronological record of all the events and all the operations carried out. The tool has various capacities, such as the production of statistics, the analysis of any modifications and operations carried out, summaries of activities performed in a specific time span, etc.

[3] *Learning objects*: Self-consistent and re-usable teaching units for e-learning. They are a particular type of digital educational resource which can be re-used in different contexts thanks to their features of modularity, re-usability, inter-operability and availability. They are base units designed to assist learning, consisting of one or more minimal elements (a video, an image, a text, etc.)

Bibliography

E- Learning

Trinchero R., *Valutare l'apprendimento nell'eLearning. Dalle abilita alle competenze*, Centro Studi Erickson, 2006

Dall'O' V., "La comunità di apprendimento nel blended learning degli insegnanti: epicentro dei flussi di sapere", *I quaderni di Form@re* n. 32, 2005

Ligorio M. B., Hermans H. (eds.), *Identita dialogiche nell'era digitale*, Trento, Erikson, 2005

Majorana C., Sgarbossa L., Salomoni V., *Nuove figure e nuovi ruoli nella formazione universitaria*, Atti expo e-learning, 2005

Pettinari E. L., Rotta M., "Ambienti sincroni in Open Source", in *Form@re* n.33, February 2005

Ranieri M., *E-learning: modelli e strategie didattiche*, Trento, Erickson, 2005

Rotta M., "L'accessibilita e l'usabilita delle piattaforme Open Source", in *Form@re* n.33, Erickson, February 2005

Spadaro P.F., Cesareni D., "Blended setting, blended learning e blended assessment, Un caso universitario", in *Form@re* n. 39, 2005

Badrul H. K., *eLearning: progettazione e gestione*, Trento, Erickson, 2004

Prece J., Rogers Y. e Sharp H., *Interaction design*, Apogeo, 2004

Rivoltella P.C., *Monitoraggio e valutazione dell'e-learning*, lecture notes Cepad, Un.Cattolica, Milan, 2004

Tellia B. (a cura di), *eLearning: strumenti e modelli per la formazione*, Forum, 2004

Anzalone F., Caburlotto F., *eLearning, comunicare e formarsi online*, Lupetti, 2003

Ardizzone P., Rivoltella P. C., *Didattiche per l'eLearning*, Carocci, 2003

Calvani A., Rotta M., *Comunicazione e apprendimento in Internet - Didattica costruttivistica in rete*, Erickson, 2003

Galliani L., Costa R., *Valutare l'eLearning*, Pensa Multimedia, 2003

COM (2002) 751 final, 19.12.2003, *Proposal for a decision of the EP and the Council adopting a multi-annual programme (2004-06) for the effective integration of Information and Communication Technologies (ITC) in education and training systems in Europe.*

COM (2002) 263 final, 28.5.2002, *Piano d'azione eEurope 2005: una societa dell'informazione per tutti*, Comunicazione della Commissione delle Comunita Europee.

COM (2001) 172 final, 28.3.2001, *The e-learning Action Plan - Designing tomorrow's education.*

ASFOR Lettera Asfor n.3/2002. "Il pianeta e-learning e le proposte Asfor: dalle Guide Lines al Glossario", in *ASFOR 2002*

Elia G., Murgia G., "Collaborative Learning. Sistemi P2P, tecnologie open source e virtual learning community" in *Informatica - Testi per professional*, 2008

Banzato M., *Apprendere in rete. Modelli e strumenti per l'eLearning*, Utet, 2002

Knowledge Management

Dellen.B., Maurer F., Pews G., "Knowledge-based techniques to increase the flexibility of workflow management", *Data & Knowledge Engineering* 23 (1997) 269-295

Gastinger A., Szegheo O., "Enterprise Modeling Approaches", in Rolstadas, *Andersen Enterprise Modeling: Improving Global Industrial Competitiveness*, pp. 55-69, Kluwer

Liebowitz J., *The Knowledge Management Handbook*, CRC Press; 1999

Malhotra Y., "Why Knowledge Management Systems fail", in Michael E.D. Koenig & T. Kanti Srikantaiah (eds.) *Knowledge management Lesson Learned*, Information Today Inc., 87-112, 2004.

Nonaka I, von Krogh G., Kazuo I. *Enabling Knowledge Creation*, Oxford University Press 2000

Smith R.G., Farquhar A., *The Road Ahead for Knowledge Management*, AI Magazine, Winter 2000

Tivana A, *Knowledge Management Toolkit*, Prentice Hall, New Jersey, 2002

Tsuia, E. B.J. Garnerb S. Staabc, *The role of artificial intelligence in knowledge management*, Knowledge-Based Systems 13 (2000) 235-239

Wenger E. (1998), *Communities of practice*, Cambridge University Press.

KNOWLEDGE REPRESENTATION

Corby O., Dieng R., Hebert C., *A Conceptual Graph Model for W3C Resource Description Framework*, in Proc. ICCS'2000 Darmstadt Germany

Decker S., Erdmann M., Fensel D., Studer R., "Ontobroker: Ontology based access to distributed and semi-structured information", in: Meersman et Hammergren T., *Data Warehousing: Building the Corporate Knowledge Base*, International Thomson Computer Press, 2000

Kolodner J., *Case Based Reasoning*, Morgna Kaufman, 1993

Russel S., Norvig, *Artificial Intelligence: A Modern Approach*, Prentice Hall, 2002

Stefik M., *Introduction to Knowledge Systems*, Morgan Kauffman, 1995

DESIGN MODELS AND TECHNOLOGIES

DESIGN MODELS

Johnson-Laird P. N., *Mental Models, Toward a Cognitive Science of Language, Inference, and Consciousness*, Cambridge, Cambridge University Press, 1983. Il Mulino, Bologna, 1988.

Oxman R., "Design by re-representation: a model of visual reasoning in Design", in *Design Studies*, vol. 18 n.4., 1997

Simon H.A., *Le scienze dell'artificiale* (The sciences of the artificial, Cambridge, Mass., MIT Press, 1981), Il mulino, Bologna 1988

Chandrasekaran B., "Multimodal Perceptual representation and design problem solving". Invited paper, *Visual and Spatial reasoning in design: computational and cognitive approaches*, 15-17 June 1999, MIT Cambridge, USA.

PROTOCOL ANALYSIS

De Grassi, M., Giretti, A., "Modelling Design E-Learning Environment Through Observation Of Designers", in Gero J. Eds, *Proceedings of International Workshop on Observing Designers,* Aix En Provence, France, 2005

Gero J.S.& T. Mc NeilL, "An approach to the analysis of design protocols", in *Design Studies*, vol. 19 n.4., 1998

Goldschmitdt G. , "On visual design thinking: the Kids of architecture", in *Design studies*, vol. 15, n.2. , 1994

Suwa M., Tversky B. , *What architects see in their sketches: implication for Design tools*, CHI 96, Companion Vancouver BC Canada. Case Based Design, 1996

Gero J.S. , "Design Prototypes: a knowledge representation schema for design", in *AI Magazine*, 1990

Maher, M.L., and Balachandran, B. Zhang D.M., *Case Based Reasoning in Design*, Lawrence Earlbaum, New Jersey, 1995

Mitchell W.J. , *The Logic of Architecture*, MIT Press, Cambridge, 1990

WEBSITES

E-learning section of the site *Servizio di Osservatorio Tecnologico per la Scuola* organised by the Ministero della Pubblica Istruzione.
http://www.osservatoriotecnologico.it/internet/e-learning.htm
Official site of the *Blackboard* e-learning platform
http://www.blackboard.com
Official site of the open source e-learning platform *Moodle*
http://moodle.org/
Official site of the open source e-learning platform *ADA*
http://ada.lynxlab.com
Official site of the *SABA* e-learning platform
http://www.saba.com/
Portal for *e-learning* on the Moodle platform of the *Sapienza University of Rome*
http://elearning.uniroma1.it/

The use of technological tools to mediate between methods and didactic purposes in distance education for architects

Mario Petrone

1. Introduction

Recourse to e-learning is usually made for the purposes of putting into effect economies of scale, in terms of the two complementary and convergent areas of unit costs of production and distribution and the increase in end-users.

Direct interpersonal rapport is regarded as generally more effective than that mediated through ICT, but the fact that it cannot be replicated tends to make it expensive, both from the point of view of the teaching (each new edition of a course has essentially duplicated costs) and of learning (at least because of space and time factors that impose the 'here and now' presence of the student).

Consequently, strategies that consider e-learning as a solution for reducing organisational costs are fairly widespread, with special attention given to distribution and access to didactic materials and interaction at a distance between the participants in the learning process. Particularly, it is the possible purpose of an e-learning project were to be identified (Keeton et al. 2002) in the search for *efficiency*, by reducing the space-time obstacles to the replication of a teaching situation, and the search for *effectiveness*, by improving the quality of the teaching state.

For institutions whose business is education, like, in our case, an University, and for whom e-learning can be an important means of fulfilling their mission (Moore, 1993; Piccoli, 2001; Smith et al, 2001; Syed, 2001; Trentin, 2000), these factors are the two poles of a continuum of opinion: in fact, one must aim at a reduction in costs while at the same time taking account of quality.

The use of technological tools to mediate between methods and didactic purposes gives us the opportunity to assist the learning process by re-thinking and re-defining teaching procedures.

This paper was written within the ambit of the project 'Research and experimentation in new models and information technologies for the distance training of architects' run by Sapienza Università di Roma and co-funded by PRIN in 2006, and aims to supply an overview of possible scenarios on the tools to be used according to the purposes to be pursued and the methods that are to be employed. We identify and analyse certain specific relationships between e-learning tools, the various ways of using them, the kind of interaction brought into play and the didactic purposes to which they are set.

2. The frame of reference

The various stages of planning and structuring of learning processes have differing degrees of freedom in the choice of the types and features of the different components relating to, for example, the roles of and relationships between teacher and students, the time allotted to classroom lessons and to individual work, the deductive approach or the inductive approach, the amount of interaction, space allotted to activities, etc. In the case of e-learning, the complex nature of these phases is increased when the use of technological tools is added to the traditional scenario. This means that the skills of those involved are of prime importance; even if it is taken for granted that a teacher possesses the ability to plan and teach a traditional lesson, the lack of a sound basis in didactic models and limited experience means that often the potential improvement of a teacher's performance through the use of technological tools is hampered by a lack of knowledge and even of information on the part of the said teacher.

Introducing e-learning solutions can thus be seen as a move towards increasing potential on the one hand, and making matters more complex on the other, often because of a lack of experience. We are therefore interested in making a study in depth that will lead to a kind of model capable of describing in a structured way how to plan scenarios of learning processes in e-learning mode. The aim of our work is in accordance with its premises and the context it is placed in: it is addressed to those who should make use of this technology, the teachers, to help them plan teaching situations appropriately and consciously by using the opportunities offered by ICT. Using our proposed model, the teacher will be able to organise processes using e-learning technology that will be more effective as far as the students' learning is concerned.

3. DIDACTIC MODELS AND TECHNOLOGICAL TOOLS

During the project 'Research and experimentation in new models and information technologies for the distance training of architects' certain teaching experiences were put forward that were innovative from the point of view of the methods and technology adopted. As a theoretical framework in e-learning pedagogy was lacking, no limitations were imposed on teachers as to their objectives or teaching methods, nor as to the technology they chose to adapt; in this way they could gain 'hands on' experience. In order to make evaluations from the learner's viewpoint (Huba et al, 1999; Weimer, 2002), solutions were chosen and were integrated into the existing teaching situation: activities that were not 'instead of' but 'together with' the current teaching, as has been for some time suggested in the literature (Marold et al. 2000; Tsichristzis, 1999). To provide an overview of the possible scenarios in which the tools will be used, based on the purpose to be pursued and on the methods to be adopted, we analysed both aspects, and particularly that of the didactic model and of the technological tools.

3.1 Didactic models

To identify the basic didactic models we made reference to three major paradigms of didactics (Luciano Galliani, 2002):
• rational-informational

- systemic-interactional
- constructivist-social

The rational-informational paradigm corresponds to a didactic model based on transmission, a learning process involving the simple transmission of content on one side and the simple acquisition of content on the other. The learner reads or acquires the content passively, there is little interaction between learner and teacher or between learners, and evaluation of performance is usually carried out by a series of tests.

The systemic-interactional paradigm corresponds to a co-operative didactic model. The course does not only consist of transmission and acquisition of content but involves exchanges and comparison of experiences and skills. Learning takes place in a group and each member of the group (teacher, expert, tutor, student) contributes to the activities carried out. This is the most widespread and most effective model.

The constructivist-social paradigm corresponds to a laboratory-based didactic model. Teamwork becomes central, and interaction is emphasised with the aim of creating a product by forming a learning community that can operate beyond the timescale of the course.

Using these paradigms, we can detect various types of interaction, made possible by the use of technological tools, between the elements involved in the educational process (teacher, student, computers); these types are:
- teacher – student (s)
- student (s) – student (s)
- student – computer

The didactic objectives (Badii et al, 2001; Bloom, 1956; Calvani et al. 1999) corresponding to the general objective of helping the students to learn are:
- teaching them to retrieve, organise and analyse the information (Ausubel, 1998; Trentin, 1998)
- heightening their critical sensibilities (Ausubel, 1999; Rombach, 1973; Wilson, 1996)
- stimulating active participation and collaboration between students (Cenarle et al, 2000; Gokhale, 1995; Paloff et al, 1999; Tinzmann et al, 1990)
- encouraging the putting into practice of what has been learnt theoretically (deductive approach) (Aster, 2001, Johnson et al, 1998)
- encouraging learning-by-doing (inductive approach) (Engines for Education; Gross Davis, 1993)

In Table 1 (S.Genone, C.Mari, L.Mari, 2002) each of the objectives and the relationships between them are listed; in particular:
- in the columns DIDACTIVE OBJECTIVES and TYPE OF INTERACTION are the items mentioned in the two lists above;
- in the column TYPE OF TOOL is a list of the software tools that can be used;

in the column METHOD OF USE is a description of how the tools can be used, with an indication of the spatial or temporal dimension (face to face/distance; synchronous/asynchronous mode).

Didactic Objectives	Type of interaction	Type of tool	Method of use
Teaching them to retrieve, organise and analyse information	Teacher/ student(s)	Forum	Distance – to communicate and exchange material between one encounter and the next
			Distance – to answer the FAQ's
	Student(s)/ computer	Animation	Face to face or distance- to assist students in the use of procedures
		Video Film	Face to face – for theoretical support using the presentation of evidence
		Glossary	Face to face or distance – used by the students to clarify the key concepts and examine them in detail
		Multimedia Presentation	Distance - self-study, to go over and study in depth the contents of the lesson
		Hypertext Structure	Face to face – to organise subjects and their contents available for the students on the net
			Face to face – to show links and relations between the didactic resources and to decide together a possible approach to navigation
			Face to face- to provide an overall picture of the topic, by presenting the didactic resources by means of conceptual maps
		Test	Distance – for self-assessment
			Face to face – to discuss the results together
Heightening their critical sensibilities	Teacher/ Student(s)	Forum	Face to face – to open discussions on specific theoretical topics
	Student(s)/ computer	Video Film	Face to face – to back up the theory by presenting evidence
			Face to face – to discuss a real situation and draw general conclusions from it
		Multimedia Presentation	Distance – self-study, to go over and study in depth the contents of the lesson
		Hypertext Structure	Face to face - to show links and relations between the didactic resources and to decide together a possible approach to navigation
			Face to face- to provide an overall picture of the topic, by presenting

			the didactic resources by means of conceptual maps
stimulating active participation and collaboration between students	Teacher/ student(s)	Virtual community	Face to face – for classroom management in real time during activities
			Face to face – to allow exchanges of contributions and files in real time between teachers, students and groups during guided activities
		Forum	Face to face – to open discussions on specific theoretical topics
			Face to face – to set up activities and collect in work done by the students
	Student(s)/ Student(s)	Virtual community	Face to face – to allow exchanges of contributions and files in real time between teachers, students and groups during guided activities
		Forum	Distance – to communicate and exchange material between one encounter and the next
	Student(s)/ computer	Video film	Face to face – to discuss a real situation and draw general conclusions from it
		Simulation business/ game	Face to face – to apply what has been presented from a theoretical viewpoint
			Face to face – to start from a concrete problem and reach the theory behind it
		Test	Distance – for self-assessment
			Face to face – to discuss the results together
encouraging the putting into practice of what has been learnt theoretically (deductive approach)	Student(s)/ computer	Animation	Face to face or distance - to assist students in the use of procedures
		Practical activities	Face to face or distance – to apply what has been presented from a theoretical viewpoint
		Video film	Face to face – to back up the theory by presenting evidence
		Simulation business/ game	Face to face – to apply what has been presented from a theoretical viewpoint
encouraging learning-by-doing (inductive approach)	Student(s)/ Computer	Practical activities	Face to face or distance – to apply what has been presented from a theoretical viewpoint
			Face to face – to start from a concrete problem and reach the theory behind it
		Video film	Face to face – to discuss a real situation and draw general conclusions from it
		Simulation business/ game	Face to face – to start from a concrete problem and reach the theory behind it

3.2 Technological tools

The e-learning tools use can often perceive a contextual inconsistency and this particular technological inconsistency deriving from the band available, from a greater amount of familiarity, from an increase in the use of 'small pieces loosely joined' and also a methodological unevenness deriving from the content, the interactions and the integration into daily life. To restrict these inconsistencies one must plan each operation:
- with a broad approach to the mix of technologies and the integration of the various tools;
- with attention paid to the tools used each day by the users.
  It is also necessary to analyse the various uses to be made of the technological tools for:
- the collaborative construction of contents;
- the sharing of materials;
- the structuring of knowledge.

Thus one should obtain the following information for each software tool to be used:
- **Purpose**
- **Main function** (communication/collaboration/sharing/structuring of knowledge)
  Secondary function (communication/collaboration/sharing/structuring of knowledge)
- **Type of interaction** (synchronous/asynchronous – one to one, many to many)
- **Prevailing type of content** (text, audio, multimedia)
- **Level of training required** (high/medium/low)
- **Potential for complex use** (high/medium/low)
- **Technological difficulty**
- **For the client** (high/medium/low)
- **For the server** (high/medium/low)
- **Running difficulties** (high/medium/low)
- **Level of transmission** (high/medium/low)
- **Costs** (high/medium/low)

Table 2 shows a chart to be used for evaluating the software solutions outlined above. There follows some examples of completed charts evaluating the following systems: wiki, blog, skype and web-conference.

4. A MODEL OF POSSIBLE SCENARIOS OF THE USE OF E-LEARNING TOOLS

Basing ourselves on our considerations of the didactic models and technological tools, we can propose the following model for identifying the scenario of the tools to be used according to the purpose to be pursued and on the methods to be adopted. On the basis of the information in Table 1, and in particular:
- Didactic purpose
- Type of interaction
- Type of tool

- Method of use
- one can identify the available software solutions that can be analysed using the factors listed in Table 2.

5. CONCLUSIONS

Using the model described this paper has shown that the different methods of use of the same software tool can correspond to different didactic purposes; the proper planning of a didactic itinerary involves not only the simple choice of tool (as frequently is the case) but also involves a complex choice of the specific ways in which one intends to use the tool. Thanks to the model we have proposed, the stages of planning and structuring learning processes, which can be ascribed to one or more of the transversal objectives we have analysed, can be read in terms of interactions and methods of use of the tools, if we plan the teaching context in different ways each time. By following the reference framework outlined here the teacher can identify the scenarios of the use of technological tools, and subsequently create teaching situations, which, by exploiting the opportunities offered by technology, will be potentially more effective by student's learning point of view. The experience derived from the use of the model may also increase the awareness among teachers of the didactic advantages offered by the adoption of ICT.

BIBLIOGRAPHY

Badii A., Truman S. (2001), "Cognitive Factors in Interface Design: An E-Learning Environment for Memory Performance and Retention Optimisation", in: Remenyi D. and Brown A., (eds), *Eighth European Conference on Information Technology Evaluation*, Oriel College, United Kingdom, 479-490.

Bloom B., *Taxonomy of Educational Objectives, Handbook 1: Cognitive Domain*, Davis McKay Lo Inc, New York, 1956.

Calvani A., Varisco B.M., eds, *Costruire/decostruire significati. Ipertesti, micromondi e orizzonti formativi*, CLUEP, Padua, 1995.

Calvani A., Rotta M., *Comunicazione e apprendimento in Internet. Didattica costruttivistica in rete*, Centro Studi Erickson, 1999.

Cenarle M., Biolghini D., *Net learning – Imparare insieme attraverso la rete*, Etas, Milan, 2000.

Dede C. (1990), *The Evolution of Distance Learning: Technology – mediated Interactive Learning, Journal of Research on Computing in Education*, 22, 3.

Engines for Education, Learning by doing, available at: http://www.engines4ed.org/hyperbook/nodes/NODE-120-pg.html

Gokhale A.A. (1995), "Collaborative Learning Enhances Critical Thinking" in *Digital Library and Archives, Journal of Technology Education*, 7, 1, Fall 1995, available at: http: //scholar.lib.vt.edu/ejournals/JTE/jte-v7n1/gokhale.jte-v7n1.html

Gross Davis B., *Tools for Teaching*, Jossey-Bass Publishers, San Francisco, 1993.

Keeton M., Sheckley B., Krejci-Griggs J., *Effectiveness and Efficiency in Higher Education for Adults*, Council on Adult and Experiential Learning, Kendall-Hunt, Chicago, 2002.

Jacobson M.J. (1994), "Issues in Hypertext and Hypermedia Research: Toward a Framework for Linking Theory-to-Design", in *Journal of Educational Multimedia and Hypermedia*, 3, 2, 1994, 141-154.

Johnson D.W., Johnson R.T., Smith K.A., *Active Learning: Cooperation in the College Classroom*, 2nd ed., Interaction Book Company, Edina, MN, 1998.

Laeng M. (1996), "La multimedialità da ieri a domani", in *Rivista dell'istruzione*, 6, 1996, 905.

Maragliano R., *Nuovo manuale di didattica multimediale*, Bari, Laterza,1998.

Piccoli G., Ahmad R., Ives B. (2001), *Web-Based Virtual Learning Environments: A Research Framework and a Preliminary Assessment of Effectiveness in Basic IT Skills Training*, MIS Quarterly, 25, 4, December 2001, 401-426.

Saunders P., Werner K. (2000), *Finding the right blend for effective learning*, Center for Teaching and Learning, Western Michigan University, available at: http://www.wmich.edu/teachlearn/new/blended.htm

Tinzmann M.B., Jones B.F., Fennimore T.F., Bakker J., Fine C., Pierce J., *What Is the Collaborative Classroom?*, NCREL, Oak Brook, 1990, available at: http://www.ncrel.org/sdrs/areas/rpl_esys/collab.htm

Trentin G., *Insegnare e apprendere in rete*, Zanichelli, Bologna, 1998.

Trentin G. (2000), "Lo Spettro dei Possibili Usi delle Reti nella Formazione Continua e a Distanza", in: *Lettera Asfor, Offerta Formativa Technology Based: Linee di Sviluppo e Criteri di Qualità*, Milan, 1-6.

Tsichristzis D. (1999), *Reengineering the University, Communications of the ACM*, 42: 6, 93-100.

Weigel V. (2000), *E-Learning and the Trade-off Between Richness and Reach* in *Higher Education, Change, The Magazine of Higher Learning*, available at:

http: //www.heldref.org/html/body_chg.html
Weimer M., Learner-Centered Teaching: *Five Key Changes to Practice*, Jossey-Bass, 2002.
Wilson B.G., *Constructivistic Learning Environments, Educational Technology Publications*, Englewood Cliffs, N.J., 1996.

Blended learning

ANNA IRENE DEL MONACO

1. A PROGRESS REPORT ON E-LEARNING: SOME REFLECTIONS

From the end of the nineties to the first decade of the twenty-first century the enthusiasm for the World Wide Web led many academics and observers to forecast the gradual replacement of traditional universities with completely virtual institutions of tertiary education.

Joergen Bang, Director of the Department of Information and Media Studies at the Aarhus University of Denmark, and president from 2002 to 2005 of the European Association of Distance Teaching Universities (*http://www.eadtu.nl/*), in two papers[1] addressed some of the issues analysed in this paragraph, i.e. the current state of distance teaching, and presented an interesting viewpoint. In this paragraph, therefore, we shall return to certain passages of Bang's papers, adding any necessary comments and references to the work of other experts that we feel are useful in describing the current state of affairs, within the terms of the project *'Research and experimentation in new models and information technologies for the distance training of architects'*.

The United States

At the end of the twentieth century, various administration boards of a number of American universities found themselves the target of unscrupulous businessmen in the education market. For example, Michael Milken, the king of 'junk-bonds', a form of high-yield 'garbage' securities, in 1997 founded the *Knowledge Universe* - he was certain he could bring historic institutions like New York's Columbia University to their knees, according to his idea that education was the currency of the third millennium, and that the administrators of prestigious universities were sitting on incalculable riches that they were totally unaware of [2]. Other experts in the same period foresaw that universities were destined to expire and become content providers to for-profit producers of 'learning-ware'.

In the same period several American universities set up commercial enterprises, alone or in collaboration with other universities, cultural institutions and e-solution providers. For example, New York University invested $20 million in *NYU Online*, Columbia $40 million to set up *Fathom* along with another 14 institutions (universities, libraries and museums). None of these universities ever launched an e-learning course[3]. Cornell University had poured $12 million into *eCor-*

nell without gaining a significant number of students. The UK Open University failed in its attempt to sell teaching products on the American market, and made a loss of around $20 million. One of the few institutions providing e-learning to succeed was the University of Phoenix, which aimed its courses at a limited and specialised market close at hand, that of business and healthcare[4].

Recently also in Italy, in the health sector, on-line degree courses for paramedical personnel have had considerable success, due to the fact that they have allowed hospital employees all over the country to obtain a first-level degree, and thus enable them to further their careers as well as provide them with personal satisfaction.

In the USA, therefore, one could say that e-learning courses have proliferated especially in the promotion of short informal 'just-in-time and just-in place' courses, while the ancient prestigious universities like Columbia, Harvard or Yale continue to be the last strongholds of Humboldtian and Kantian thought, giving to the new technologies mere supporting roles and combining them with traditional teaching.

Europe

In this same period, with the indisputable success of the internet, the European Council approved the setting up of an extremely important programme, *eEurope*, whose aim was to create "an information society for all" (Lisbon, March 2000) and to promote, by 2010, "the most competitive and dynamic knowledge-based economy in the world". In March 2000 the European Commission published a communication entitled '*e-Learning – Designing the education of tomorrow*'[5].

Alongside these political initiatives but without any coordination on the part of the European Commission, several national and European e-learning projects were launched: the e-University in Britain (UKeU), the Digital University in the Netherlands, the Bavarian Virtual University, the Virtual University in Finland and the Net-University in Sweden. Among the inter-institutional experiments we can mention WINDS: Web-based INtelligent Design tutoring System, which brought together various working groups from ten European countries in an attempt to set up a virtual university for the teaching of architectural design. Five years later, the UKeU had ceased operations: the global successor to the Open University in the 21st century had never attracted financial backing from business partners and had recruited only 900 students instead of the expected 5000. The operation cost £60 million in public funds. The Dutch Digital Universiteit - a consortium of universities in the Netherlands, along with IT sector firms and publishing houses – never achieved a significant number of customers, and partners are thinking of pulling out of the consortium. The Virtual University of Finland and the Swedish Net-University, both government-backed, have increased the number of courses on-line, in an attempt to attract students from other institutions and regions in the country, but the much-expected collaboration with other institutions has so far failed to appear. The Virtual University of Bavaria (vhb),

another government-run enterprise, has successfully increased the already substantial number of e-learning courses available to students from all Bavarian universities, without any significant result being apparent along the lines of improved inter-institutional collaboration.[6]

WINDS is the only initiative at a European level to have produced an inter-European architecture course entirely on-line and thus can be used as a guideline for on-line teaching applied to architecture, extremely useful for further research and to examine the reasons for its recognised lack of success in certain areas. The most important lesson to be learnt from the general failure of European virtual universities and the e-learning experiences mentioned above, is that none of them reached a level of sustainability, in the sense of the capacity to attract users, to finance themselves and be competitive on the education market; without government backing, none of them can survive.[7]

As well as reporting on the lack of success of the virtual university projects, Bang in his two papers introduces the problem of blended learning. Reading what Bang has written and comparing his views with those of other academics, we can say that the Lisbon conference of 2000 can be seen in a certain sense as a form of watershed between the first generation of e-learning products, those which featured learning objects and which treated e-learning mostly as a cognitive issue, and the second generation, which uses Web 2.0 software.

The first generation used e-learning above all as a pedagogic tool and investigated the paradigms of teaching design by means of semantic technologies[8] and the networking structure of knowledge[9].

The second generation, on the other hand, uses as auxiliaries mixed tools of the Web 2.0 type: Wikipedia, yahoo, youtube, twitter, social networks, blogs, etc.

1.
The AADVD platform created by the Architectural Association of London.

In considering the validity of the first generation products, Professor Bang points to a 2001 report by the OECD (Organisation for Economic Cooperation and Development) which highlights the difficulties in successfully carrying through e-learning experiments: "In spite of having spent $16 billion in 1999 in OECD countries on ICT[10], there is (...) no conclusive evidence that ICT investments made by the public sector have resulted in improved performance of teachers and/or learners, nor that there has been an improvement in quality and in access to educational resources on the scale predicted" (*e-learning, the Partnership Challenge*, 2001, p. 24).

A later report by the OECD in 2005, *e-learning in Tertiary Education: Where do we stand?* maintains that the new technologies have certainly improved the management processes of learning, but not its quality or its contents.

"e-learning has not really revolutionised learning and teaching to date. Far-reaching, novel ways of teaching and learning, facilitated by ICT, remain nascent or still to be invented (...) The adoption of learning management systems (LMS) (...) appears to be one of the prominent features of e-learning development in tertiary education worldwide. (...) the current immaturity of online learning is demonstrated by the low adoption of content management systems (...) ICT has penetrated tertiary education, but has had more impact on administrative services (e.g. admissions, registration, fee payment, purchasing) than on the pedagogic fundamentals of the classroom" (*e-learning in Tertiary Education. Where do we stand?*, 2005, p. 14-15).

Developing countries are a case apart, especially in Africa, where distance learning is regarded as an extremely important resource since it gives access to education to a considerable number of people who would otherwise have no alternative. E-learning is thus a tool that helps guarantee equal rights, and in fact UNESCO lends strong support to programmes set up for this purpose.

One key figure in the management and promotion of e-learning is *European Commissioner for Information and Media* Viviane Reding[11]. At a forum held in Karlsruhe in 2003, when the WINDS project had just finished, she said:

"Modern e-learning solutions now recognise the importance of learning as a social process and offer possibilities for collaboration with other learners, for interaction with the learning content and for guidance from teachers and tutors. (...) Once more, teachers and tutors play a central role, using virtual and face to face interaction with their students in a **'blended' approach**. An approach in which they are no longer seen simply as **consumers of pre-determined e-learning content** but as **editors, authors and contributors** to a contextualised learning scenario."

Bang cautions against interpreting Reding's words as a total lack of confidence in e-learning and learning objects, but instead to see them as an invitation to develop forms of blended learning that are better integrated and involve more responsibility on the part of both teachers and students in the learning process.

The e-learning solutions that have been the leading experimenters with mixed material have been the **Open Uni-**

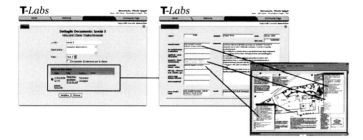

versities, especially the Open University of the United Kingdom (UKOU) and the MIT Open Courseware Consortium (*http://www.ocwconsortium.org/*). The aims of the Open Universities are to integrate learning activities, materials and tutorials into a blended learning process and to make sure that the activities are culturally relevant. The Open University platforms have collections of documents which could be said to correspond to traditional university printed lecture notes, ordered according to the timetable of the course. It is, therefore, a somewhat traditional learning tool transmitted on the net, and the documents are a form of publication that can be consulted as one follows the course programme.

In an interesting passage, J. Bang highlights one of the main risks that e-learning projects can run:

"Viewing learning, and especially e-learning, as a **process of knowledge transfer instead of knowledge construction**; too much emphasis has been placed on the concept of stand-alone courses and resource-based learning. (...) My point is not to diminish the achievements of the learning object concept, but to question the concept of learning, which in many cases is incorporated through instructional design theory. This is based on 'the empiric assumption that **behaviour is predictable**, and that educational design, therefore, can occur in isolation from educational execution' (Koper, 2000, p. 14), but '(...) a lot of learning does not come from knowledge resources at all, but stems from the activities of learners solving problems, interacting with real devices, interacting in their social and work situation (...) it is the activities of the learners in the learning environment which are accountable for the learning' (Koper, 2001, p. 3)"[12]

Thus the logical transition from the first generation of e-learning products to the second, according to the viewpoints we have so far quoted, tends to remove the 'pre-packaged' nature of the first generation from that of the second. Other experts like Morten Flate Pailsen accuse the e-learning processes of being too 'industrialised', a paradoxical statement seeing that they are in fact a product of post-industrial society.

"Learning resources (learning objects) only become active during the learning process when the learner is doing something useful with them. The creation of relevant learning activities becomes essential. Successful learning activities mobilise the capacities (present knowledge, cultural heritage, etc.) of learners and establish a dialogue with the new learning resource as the basis for learning. Hereby, teachers and tutors are reinstalled in a position as responsible for organising the

2.
TDraw virtual atelier.

learning process. They are choosing relevant learning resources and creating learning activities needed in order to reach defined educational objectives."[13]

For this reason the process of knowledge building used by the Open Universities is the more effective, since it guarantees to a greater extent the production of independent critical work on the part of the learner, oriented towards the 'building' of knowledge, not only to its transmission. When Web 2.0 and Web 3.0 tools like Google Books can permit one to consult most of the books in the libraries of the world, the problem of building up resources, which was paramount for the first generation e-learning products, will be of minimal importance, on a par with the problems of traditional quality teaching: the course materials, the lessons by the teacher, etc. In this way the construction of learning objects, the data-bank of on-line courses, can be avoided, or at least reduced, since the original resources will be mostly available on the net. The students will thus have direct access to the sources, without any filter or previous selection on the part of the teacher (with the accompanying risk of creating a form of on-line 'crib').

The perfecting of techniques for consulting on-line information and the definitive transfer of traditional paper materials (books and magazines) on to the web – real **on-line publications** and **on-line archives**[14] – will revolutionise the learning process much more than a custom-made interface ever could, using pre-packaged learning objects.

The most reliable systems for distance education, therefore, today tend to use as much as possible the software and open-source platforms available on the market, integrating and combining them according to the specific needs of the discipline and the courses, applying them alongside traditional teaching, that is, the direct teacher-student rapport, which is not pre-packaged but assisted and supported by the technological innovations to be found on the market.

2. Some study cases tried out in teaching courses in architectural design in the Faculty of architecture 'Ludovico Quaroni' of Sapienza Università di Roma, and a comparison with certain distance models and tools for architecture

Rome Sapienza began experiments with e-learning platforms with the introduction of the *Black Board* platform, which is still widely used in courses in medicine. The university subsequently expanded its experimentation by setting up a portal to the open source platform Moodle, which was run by professional programmers and at the disposal of the whole university. In July 2009 the Rector, Luigi Frati, inaugurated a structure to manage a certain number of e-learning courses called TELMA SAPIENZA. Rome Sapienza's experience of distance education, therefore, takes various forms: commercial platforms, open source platforms, and e-learning courses.

Here we are referring to officially established systems open to the whole university, which do not include a certain number of on-line courses independently managed by teachers (like the optional course *Design on-line* run by Professor Belibani in the L. Quaroni Faculty, an outcome of the WINDS project, or the *Post Graduate Course – E-learning – Overview to IT Revolution* in Architecture within the ambit of the European project for post-graduate courses *e.archidoct* run by Professor Antonino Saggio), as well as many other courses run in association with other organisations such as Omiacom, the Marconi Telematic University, or run in tandem with some faculties and other private organisations.

In the PRIN project the choice of a work platform posed some difficulties. The Research Unit (RU) of Rome Sapienza chose an open source product, Moodle, after lengthy discussions with the Molise Unit run by Professor Mario Petrone, and after a detailed examination of the uncertain results of the WINDS project, in which various members of the research units had taken part.

One must keep in mind the fact that the application of e-learning products to architecture, and in particular to architectural design, which was traditionally taught by working in an *atelier*, is difficult to effect with any degree of success; that is, in being able to show that the use of distance teaching guarantees better results than those obtained by traditional courses.

The Moodle platform was tried out as an auxiliary tool integrated into traditional teaching, for two successive academic years, in the following design courses: Exhibition Design laboratory, academic year 2007/2008 (taught by Anna Del Monaco, course topic "info-point in the Colle Oppio park"), Final Synthesis laboratory, 2007/2008 (taught by Lucio Barbera and Anna Del Monaco, course topic: "residential settlement at Tenuta della Crocetta, Pomezia"), Final Synthesis laboratory 2008/2009 (taught by Lucio Barbera and Anna Del Monaco, course topic: "residential settlement at Casal di Gregna, Rome"), Thesis Seminar, 2008/2009 (taught by Lucio Barbera and Anna Del Monaco, Seminar topic "residential settlement and services at Sheoku, Shenzhen, China).

In their initial stage, the courses using Moodle, parallel to the traditional courses, aimed to set up real adaptive learning environments and to become the theoretical critical tool for the entire course, both in their ability to organise the contents and to evaluate the results. Only where a distinct improvement in quality can be proved to have taken place in the teaching of architectural design can one speak of innovation brought about by the use of such tools, apart from their obvious capacity to resolve and simplify practical and organisational problems and to coordinate the teaching; one positive point in fact emerges: almost all the students take the exam in the first session. Thus apart from learning objects (documents .doc, .PPT, http//, .pdf, .jpg), course structures (calendar, deadlines, consignments on-line), course indexes (links to theoretical contents internal and external to the Moodle platform), and feedback and recommendation areas (forum, assessments, chat), in other words the standard e-learning tools of the first generation, we explored the possibility of modifying the standard functions of the open source product, Moodle, partially and gradually adding to it certain functions offered by other digital platforms custom made by some avant-garde internationally renowned schools of architecture.

The AADVD platform for instance, created by the Architectural Association of London (fig. 1) and the MIT website were an important point of reference for our adapting the chosen open source platform to enable us to organise an on-line exhibition of the students' work, in order to show the trend in educational production of the school and contribute to the formation of the school's 'modus', its average behaviour.

The London school's Digital Research Laboratory gave us the idea of using our 'modified' open source platform to update the theoretical design contributions of the teachers and the work of the students throughout the academic year, with the idea of using it not only as a tool for disseminating information but also as a comparative assessment of the teaching activities carried out.

However, the Moodle platform showed a lack of flexibility in the more innovative areas; we managed to set up **adaptive learning environments** for **blended learning**, even if these were created according to the logic of graphic templates rather than that of the perfectly custom made version on the London AA website; we also had the possibility of organising the Course Portfolio and a database of graphic and theoretical contributions outside of the Moodle platform.

The limitations of Moodle were also found in other requirements specific to the teaching of design: the need to read CAD files and make corrections directly on the files inside the platform[15], and to set up and organise quickly slide shows and databases (lessons or student consignments) without having to upload the files one by one, as was the case with Moodle. These tools, however, could be included in an e-mailbox where a text can be edited and also a pen or pencil tool can be used, like that found in graphic software.

In any case, a number of other surveys of the features of alternative software packages, both commercial and open-source, showed that this inflexibility was shared by many. In the case of Moodle, Rome Sapienza has, at our suggestion, officially set up an experimental programme entrusted to a team of software designers which backs up and updates the on-line activities within university courses. This is an extremely important support system, since the platform is already set up and ready for use in the course. The version Moodle 2 is expected shortly, into which we asked the designers to include the adaptations that we tried out (with mixed tools), especially the possibility of using *ePortfolio* and tools with which results can be shown and compared.

We have therefore to make a compromise between the possibility of having at our disposal ready-to-use open source platforms (as is the case with blogs like *eblogger* and *wordpress*), and custom made platforms which, once set up and activated, are already obsolete compared with the commercial products. The learning times however, in my opinion, are the real novelty in the use of these tools. Architectural design laboratories in traditional teaching usually take place on a weekly or twice weekly basis. In some cases, with a greater commitment on the part of the teacher, distance education tools can be used for intermediate checks that speed up and improve the students' progress on the project. This was unthinkable some years ago: after a week or a fortnight, if the project went wrong one had to wait another week for it to be corrected.

These tools speed up and improve learning and with obvious differences recall the old system of ex-tempore classroom lessons, even if they are spread over more days with the use of up to date technologies.

In the courses where Moodle was used, the lack of flexibility was compensated for by the use of on-line tools that were not part of the platform (of Web 2.0 type) as mentioned above. Flickr (www.Flickr.com) a social utility network run by Yahoo in particular showed interesting functions such as the organisation of a database of images which was very useful when integrated with Moodle for the collective presentation of the partial and final results of the course, and also for an on-going comparative evaluation of the results of the teaching. In fact, in the specific area of architectural design, by convention and by tradition, the assessing of students is always comparative and for teaching purposes a comparison of the products of the course is indispensible (the course Portfolio). In the thesis seminar mentioned above (Shenzhen) for reasons of flexibility it was decided to give all the participants, whether teachers or students, the role of 'teachers' (fig. 3); this was the only way for everyone to take part with equal roles, to have the authority to explore the platform, upload external resources and, much more importantly, to be able to compare their work with that of the others involved.

The results of the workshop 'the origins of the contemporary' organised and created by the Rome RU for the PRIN research – run over two weeks with the Synthesis Laboratory students (Profs Barbera and Del Monaco) in 2008-09, entirely online from registration to final work consignment, without any form of intermediate assessment and very few contacts on the Moodle platform – lead us to make certain observations. The notably precise construction of the learning object based on equally precise and comprehensive research documentation on the topic of 'the origin of the contemporary' and on videos of lessons and other contributions of the teachers of the Roma Tre RU does not result in any considerable improvement in quality in the work produced by the students. Some of it is interesting and intelligent, but overall it displays a certain amount of generalisation and superficiality.

Probably the problem lies in the kind of task required of the student, even though this is a task that architecture students are accustomed to deal with in traditional courses (not on-line). Or perhaps the problem of superficiality derives from the risks inherent in mass culture, in its worst form, which a type of pre-packaged learning certainly does not help to alleviate.

In conclusion, one can say that the many and varied experiences gained by the use of Moodle and Web 2.0 tools have allowed us to clarify which are the principal, essential requirements for the creation of a type of platform that can be used for distance teaching in architecture, taking into consideration the current level of technology:

The possibility of creating (on the part of both teachers

and students) a versatile collection (slide show) of a large number of images, for creating databanks and ePortfolios, which, as we said above, help to create a 'modus'of cultural behaviours.

The development and updating of specialised tools for software used by architects, to be integrated into generic platforms as 'default' features.

The designing of ever more efficient tools for communication in chat and the transfer of data and files between teachers and students.

NOTES

[1] Joergen Bang: (1) *Beyond blended learning! Undiscovered potentials for e-learning in organizational learning* and (2) e-*Learning reconsidered. Have e-learning and virtual universities met the expectations?* Source: www.elearningeuropa.info (2006)

[2] See Mark Taylor, *The Moment of Complexity: Emerging Network Culture* (2003)

[3] This of course applies to the situation at the time; today, instead, e-learning courses are offered alongside traditional courses and act as back-up for extra-curricular activities.

[4] Joergen Bang. *Ibid.*

[5] *http://eur-lex.europa.eu/LexUriServ/LexUriServ.do?uri=COM:2001:0172:FIN:IT:PDF*

[6] This data is carefully described by Joergen Bang (2). *Ibid.*

[7] Joergen Bang (2). *Ibid.*

[8] Semantic technology: the basic concept behind semantic technology is that of understanding the meaning of contents in order to be able to manage knowledge at a conceptual level (and no longer by means of key-words), in ways similar to those employed by people. If, for example, we want to know in which films two actors appeared together, we can look up Wikipedia or IMDB and find the answer, but only after spending quite some time reading and comparing a certain amount of irrelevant information; with semantic technology, all we have to do is ask a question to get an immediate answer. Similarly, we can find all the documents where the word 'automobile' is associated with 'energy-saving' simply by choosing these two concepts from the list provided. The problem is: how can we achieve this? Experts in the field who took part in the Semantic Technology Conference 2007 (established firms, start-ups, and new internal developments in businesses previously not part of the sector) have various ways of approaching the galaxy of the semantic management of knowledge, inevitably given the enormously complex nature of the problem. The simplest, most classic and common approach is to create ontologies of concepts, generic or specific to one sector, that can be used to label contents (manually or automatically) with conceptual tags: if the ontology indicates that 'station wagon' is a hyponym of 'automobile', and if we attach the 'automobile' tag to a document, we will then also find the documents that deal only with station wagons without ever mentioning the word automobile. (Marco Varone, il sole 24 ore 06/07/07 Nova 100)

[9] Giovanni Adorni, Mauro Coccoli, Gianni Vercelli, Giuliano Vivanet, *Un modello semantico di progettazione di contenuti didattici in ambienti di e-learning*, Source: *http://siel08.cs.unitn.it/Atti/lavori/adorni1.pdf*

[10] Information and Communication Technologies

[11] Viviane Reding has been prominent in the setting up of the new generation of Socrates programmes in the educational field and has supported the development, distribution and promotion of audio-visual products in Europe, by studying innovative methods for promoting the circulation of films and the drawing up of rules for national governments for assistance in the film-making sector.

[12] Joergen Bang (2). *Ibid.*

[13] Joergen Bang (2). *Ibid.*

[14] Franca Bossalino, Researcher in the Department of Architecture DiAR of Rome Sapienza, has collected her recent researches into Sustainable Architecture in a databank that can be consulted on the web, in collaboration with the LaMA Multimedia Laboratory for Architecture; the site, *http://w3.uniroma1.it/diarambiente*, is continually updated and is extremely useful both for research and for teaching.

[15] Vittorio Spigai, Massimiliano Condotta and Elisa Dalla Vecchia of the Istituto Universitario IUAV of Venice experimented in 2003 with systems called WITarch (knowledge storage and implementation system), TDraw *virtual atelier* (fig. 2).

POLITECNICO DI TORINO
DIPARTIMENTO DI PROGETTAZIONE
ARCHITETTONICA E DISEGNO INDUSTRIALE
Head of research unit: Liliana Bazzanella

Research unit:

Gustavo Ambrosini
Marilù Barelli
Mauro Berta
Michele Bonino
Luca Caneparo
Pierre-Alain Croset
Massimo Crotti
Giovanni Durbiano
Francesco Guerra
Elena Masala
Alfonso Montuori
Stefano Pensa
Luca Reinerio
Giuseppe Roccasalva

Learning from Designing Cities in Silico

LILIANA BAZZANELLA
LUCA CANEPARO

INTRODUCTION

There is a surprise in the end credits of the film *Chain*, directed by Jem Cohen, when we discover that the anonymous places where the film was shot, shopping malls, single-family houses, business premises, car parks, on the sides of streets and highways, were filmed in seven different countries. Although none of them were shot in Italy, it is not difficult to recognise the same kind of mixture of buildings we can find along our roads. The director uses these places not only as background to his characters; it is the plot itself that is modular: the sections of narrative are interchangeable and can be rearranged by the spectator to make new sequences, even new films. Similarly, the places filmed can be infinitely replicated along the roads to create identical landscapes: from the Astigiano to Zuid-Holland (Fig. 1)

The question is: how did this happen?

The majority of these buildings were designed; they received building permits, following regulatory plans and town planning schemes. And yet there was no overall design, no inclusive plan, either of the surroundings or at a social level, or on the level of daily life, shared by all the actors in the 'real'-film. What does this tell us? In western society, an individual who builds his own house or the multinational that constructs a shopping mall both play an important role in defining the nature of a place. Also, the sum of the parts produces a comprehensive result, which is different from both individual and public plans of how to govern the territory.

THE ASSUMPTIONS OF THE RESEARCH

Our research originated in the observation that the design tools normally used in urban transformations encounter problems, in that the large number and different kinds of requirements imposed by the market, by initiatives, by communication, tend to question the relationship between the design and the plan.

What answer can research provide today to the question of which tools are available to teachers and students – the technicians, politicians and citizens of the future – that can be used to design extensive sections of cities, in the complexity of their relationship with the environment, in the intricate interrelations with the needs of production, services, housing and commerce, with economic, demographic, social, infrastructural and environmental dynamics? The spread of these phenomena and

1.
Aligned along arteries mixture of activities and spaces that can be recombined into different lanscapes, yet always looking the same.

their non-linear inter-relationships has, in the best of cases, been dealt with by setting up workshop or charrette for the purpose of bringing together citizens and decision-makers and the different skills of authorities. In Piedmont the Regional Law N°1 of 20 February 2007 prescribes 'conferences of planning' for the procedures of authorising 'structural variations' to the Regulatory Plans. These conferences must allow communities and local authorities to discuss together any topics proposed as variations on regional plans, above the local level.

Whatever the urban legislation in force, in Italy, as in Europe and the USA, decisions on the uses of the territory tend to be taken at a local level, at that of the municipality, for example. The government's responsibility for creating opportunities tends to express itself at a local level, by defining which areas should be developed for housing, commerce, services or industry. Local administrations can claim that the offers of areas and the increase in activities can become a drive for local development, both in terms of producing welfare capital, either from taxes or reinvestment in infrastructure, such as public transport or services. Yet these infrastructure systems are not entirely manageable at the local level: roads and main communication routes, railways, multi-modal systems and large scale transport operate at a regional or higher scale. Here local administrations are pushed to give up their authority and delegate everything to a supposed self-regulating capability of the market, in conjunction with to national or supra-national plan for infrastructures. This, not altogether paradoxically, multiplies the role of the architect in the design, which becomes a plug, a self-contained unit of meaning, in a territory without any choerence, a meaning at a higher scale. Vice versa, when designs are at local scale, they tend to express and communicate the intentions and interests of groups who are aiming to make use of the territory. Large scale projects for Milan or Paris, for example, are paradigms of these inclinations expressed as designs: the location, density and intended use of areas of expansion subject to a change in function, of services, parks and public spaces, allow us to understand the majority structures in Administrations and in economic groups.

THE OBJECT OF THE RESEARCH

Our research experimented with innovative methods and technologies for urban and regional design, using integrated micro-simulation models, with the aim of comparing different possible scenarios of territorial development and mobility layout. We analysed how development paths might be modified at a metropolitan or regional scale so that the the designs of the transformations could be matched with general aims taken as guidelines – the design scenarios. Simulation of the scenarios is in fact a way of checking for deviations and contradictions and initiating potential processes of open learning.

The process is based on a consensual and cooperative governance system that has been widely tested in Italy and abroad. In the USA governance at a regional scale 'involves voluntary horizontal cooperation, and is superior to regional government, which entails formal institutions that regulate vertically.' (Savitch, 2000). The experience of the Strategic Plan of Turin suggests that the adoption of a participatory governance comes into conflict in practice with usual forms of decision making, and that participants tend to compete with one another for primacy, rather than cooperate together. Local experiences attest to the daily difficulties due to conflicting demands of the people concerned, caused by frictions produced by putting projects into practice at a urban scale, which are aimed at programming for the future and the making of complex urban policies.

Our research demonstrates the central role of design and technological disciplines in the new role driven by micro-simulation stimulates in the designand palnning practices, within a new inter-disciplinary framework that aims at interpreting the complex nature of urban dynamics over time. Our Research Unit's experiments were aimed at examining in detail the potential provided by technology to support large scale designs, exploring the morphological aspects of the spatial construction of scenarios and placing them at the beginning of the process, contextually to policy and government processes. We esteem this an added value of our research and experimentation, both for the practiceand for the teaching of urban design.

In order to give the students of our Schools the methodological basis necessary for the morphological representation of urban scenarios, we needed to reconsider the interpretative and design instruments that are available, and from this starting point, see how their capacities could be improved. From a first non-systematic survey, it would appear that representation instruments have acquired a pre-eminence, particularly with systems of two-dimensional drawing and rendering, with standardising results that tend to restrict any competency in pre-figuration and figurative exploration. As an alternative to this cultural mono-dimensionality, our research examined the educative capabilities of *virtual laboratories*. In other disciplines these laboratories are widely employed in teaching, as well as for experimental purposes. Not only physics, mathematics or biology, but also economics, sociology, geography and engineering use simulations for teaching purposes, to explain how a process or system behaves dynamically.

THE METHODOLOGICAL BASIS

At the end of the sixties, Guy Orcutt, a researcher at Massachusetts Institute of Technology, came up with the idea of simulation models at the level of single individuals. He called them micro-simulations, because they represented the population individually, in terms of census data, such as age, sex, education, income, etc. At first these models were used to simulate socio-economic dynamics, incomes or taxation policies. Later micro-simulation models began to represent explicitly geographical data, by locating workplaces,residences or activities. In the seventies there was a growing disillusionment with the models: they needed too much data, too many resources, and their validation was regarded as prohibitive (Lee, 1973). Halfway through the eighties new models of micro-simulation were developed, using new methods and technologies. An important innovation was Daniel McFadden's idea of modelling individual choices among a discrete number of possibilities. In 2000,

McFadden received the Nobel Prize in Economics 'for the development of the theory and methods of analysing discretionary choices'. Meanwhile computers increased in computing power, reducing costs. Software was invented to simulate systems made up of countless individual entities who acted independently and interacted reciprocally with one another: software agents. Also, a growing number of companies and agencies were collecting and processing scattered detailed information that was previously the domain of national censuses.

The reasons why simulation models are used in urban and regional design ground on three main factors:

In the last few decades research has begun to compete with problems that cannot be dealt with the viewpoint of a single discipline (Husserl, 1961), and that cannot be divided up and examined as separate parts or subsystems. These problems need a synthetic approach (Santa Fe Institute, 1988) which involves researchers from different fields of study. The Santa Fe Institute in the US, The Institute for Scientific Interchange Foundation in Italy and other groups have taken-chargeto overcome interdisciplinary boundaries and concentrate on new methods and techniques at the crossroads between various disciplines. Much of this work has been made possible and carried out through the use of in silicosimulation models (Waddel, 2005).

The relevant progress that has been made in the techniques of data collection and treatment, leading to a simpler way of dealing with the complex nature of the interactions involved.

A different way of assessing the performance of urban and regional design projects, and thus a different role assigned to simulation models in their preparation and operation.

Different approaches in the simulation to support the processes underlay different spatial processes, supporting different methodologies in design and decisions processes for the transformation of the city and region. The methodology that we assumed is extensive, oriented to involve the different design practices at different scales, aiming at the reconstruction of the separation between architectural design, civil engineering and planning (Ciribini, 1984, Desportes, 1997, Gabetti, 1983)

SimTorino

The *High Quality Laboratory – Integrated Territorial Project* of Politecnico di Torino[2], after five years of work, has completed the micro-scale modelling of the Turin urban area. The project was named *SimTorino*, after the video game *SimCity*: the best-selling title in the short and turbulent history of video games. SimCity is a black box in which the ideas and theories of the model are hidden – although certain conjectures have been put forward on how the simulation functions – "SimCity rests on a Keynesian hypothesis of development, according to a scheme of equilibrium between supply and demand in each sector: industrial, commercial and residential." (Caneparo, 2005).

On the other hand, the *SimTorino* model is open and publically documented: interaction between individuals is simulated by six sub-models: accessibility, economic and demographic models, mobility, location choice and development of the housing market. The model is implemented on the OPUS platform, an international project aimed at developing and promoting 'an open platform for urban simulation' (Waddel, 2005). In silico, *SimTorino* individually simulates each of the 638,785 family units, the 658,110 workers and the 107,338 buildings which, since the initial year of 2001, are to be found in the 34 Municipalites of the Turin metropolitan area (Fig. 2). It simulates the decisions about location, relocation or development of households, jobs and businesses. The model simulates the individualedifices, in order to assess the amount of supply and demand in the real estate market. It simulates the transport system and the mobility by private car or by public transport. The model is *integrated*, in that it can be used to study combinations of activities and the use of buildings with mobility, which is useful, for example, for reducing the number of critical points or axes by constructing new infrastructures, or improving the efficiency of existing ones. The integrated simulation is a potentially support tool for urban or regional decision-making.

It enables researchers to study the relationship between increased accessibility, due to new road systems, or a reduced mobility because of the higher costs or environmental impact of the transport system, or choices concerning locationing and mobility of population and business firms.

Our research aims at experimenting effectively new methodologies and technologies in urban design, using integrated micro-simulation models, so as to compare various possible scenarios of urban development and mobility organisation, by analysing how the development paths of the Turin metropolitan area can be modified, to fit projects and interventions with general objectives which have been adopted as guidelines – the design scenarios. At the same time, the research will check deviations and contradictions and thus initiate potential processes of open learning for the actors involved.

SimTorino demonstrates the important innovative nature of design and technology disciplines. Within the inter-disciplinary framework of design and planning., micro-simulation reinforces the exploration of the morphological aspects of the spatial construction of scenarios and sets them at the beginning of the process, in the context of policy and government. We esteem this is an important valid aspect of our research and experimentation, especially in the context of the more innovative experimentations being carried out at the international level. In line with the most advanced practices, for example, the *Chicago Metropolitan Plan* and the *Communities across Province of Ontario*, the Turin experiment places morphology at the centre of urban transformation: the design scenarios can become shared objectives and subjects of discussion also because they are 'forms', in other words, figurations of constructed landscapes. In the international experimentations mentioned above, the morphology was almost always eluded, whereas in SimTorino large scale design has an improved role: no longer specialising in 'form' in the context of urban design, which unfortunately frequently comes after political, technical and economical decisions, oriented by the demands imposed by the market, by initiatives, by communication, and which threaten to reduce the design into a sequence of objects, eliminating the complexities of the relationships with the urban or regional scale. Whereas SimTorino, in the scenario simulation process, the role of the architect becomes concurrent to the descriptive and implementative stages of metropolitan transformations: the role of the designer is to interpret the morphology of the city in the shaping of the transformations in an equal measure to the other contributions.

VIRTUAL LABORATORY EXPERIMENTS IN THE TEACHING OF URBAN DESIGN

Some experiments with simulation tools for the teaching of architectural design have been successfully carried out abroad, using *virtual laboratories*. Here we shall give a brief overview of these experiments at their principal scales of reference. Each experiment differed from the others and was confined to a specific scale, but we found that common to all of them were simulation tools devised to integrate design topics with multiple skills/roles in virtual laboratories. Generally speaking, the purpose was to experiment on field – learning by doing –educative design methodologies, aimed at acquiring extensive knowledge of, rather than solving, the design issues.

At the ETH Zurich in 2001, the professor of the chair of City Planning, Kees Christiaanse, and that of Computer Aided Architectural Design, professor Ludger Hovestadt, founded the Kaisersrot research group, to make detailed investigations of integrated research methods at points where architecture, design and information technology intersect. The group's objectives were to make innovations in the practice of urban design, abandoning the usual division into different scales, between urban and architectonic scales, which tended to be formulated and decided within a hierarchical framework. The Kaisersrot group experimented with information technologies to create horizontal information processing systems, based on the primary elements of the project: the software looked for the points of equilibrium between the parts, searching for stability in the countless variations in the relationships. These points of equilibrium tend towards a stable configuration which is not necessarily a morphological outcome but rather the minimum number of relationships between the parts. The group carried out a number of experiments of this design methodology into the practice, for example in collaboration with KCAP, Herzog & de Meuron and Sauerbruch & Hutton, as well as in the educational field, in semester project units at ETH.

Professor Bill Hillier at the Bartlett School in London and SpaceSyntax Ltd, from the sixties, has developed the *Space Syntax* method, which, if used properly, is both a knowledge tool and a support for designing and planning. It has been successfully tested at various scales: for urban design is advanced a syntactic model for supporting the design process. This model can interpret the social value of spatial configurations as they are utilised on a daily basis and as they represent social organisation in its physical form. The syntactic model has distinct advantages over other models in used in the practice; above all it crosses different scales, aiding the design action from the relationship between transport systems and the land use, to individual mobility and single buildings. Besides this, the model, as an knowledge tool used to interpret the functioning of the city, can be applied to simulate the outcomes of design alternatives and quickly investigate the long-term effects of different alternatives. Since the sixties these capabilities of the Space Syntax method have been tested in numerous projects, not only within the ambit of the SpaceSyntax company but also in the much larger field of the international group which has adopted the method. Similarly the experiments in the didactic field have been extended outside the Bartlett School to dozens of courses and design units all over the world.

Professor Yehuda E. Kalay of the University of California at Berkeley has created an on-line game to simulate processes that involve both collaborative and conflicting aspects of design. The aim of the game is "to simulate, exercise, and provide a feel for the social dimension of collaboration, by embedding mutual dependencies that encourage players to engage each other—in adversarial or collaborative manners—to accomplish their goals. Specifically, it is intended to help students understand what collaboration is, why it is necessary, and how it is done." (Kalay, 2003) The scale of the simulation is the suburbs, the design of single-family housing, the roles are those of customer, architect, builder and the planner, implicit in the rules laid down before the game begins. One should also remember that small communities in the USA are not required to draw up a regulatory plan.

Erez Hatna and Itzhak Benenson at the Environmental Simulation Laboratory of the University of Tel Aviv have carried out experiments, which are interesting, even if only partially relevant to virtual laboratories, using a game environment where students are asked to build a city or a part with fifty-two miniature building models. The experiment pays particular attention to the behavioural aspects of the 'planning' and tries to draw out any individual or group regularity in design strategies, even as a comparison between different students and with systems of automatic generation. The teaching method is oriented towards behavioural theories rather than the anthropological principles experimented by Schön (1987) in teaching architectural design.

Virtual laboratories of urban design

The Virtual Laboratory of urban design is aimed at allowing students to acquire an awareness of the complex interrelations between urban scenarios and morphological pre-figurations, between governance and the architectural and environmental scales of the project, and between design and decision-making processes: they learn from the outcomes of their design scenarios, simulated in the temporal dimension.

We are convinced that the virtual laboratory experiments mentioned above, even those in other disciplines such as biology, economics, physics, geography, informatics, engineering, mathematics or sociology, draw attention to various methodological effects that are potentially relevant for the teaching of urban design. Generally, the various disciplines devise simulations to teach how a process or a system works by means of experience – learning by doing. Methodologically, the various experiences of virtual laboratories encourage the students to:
• develop their own understanding of the phenomenon

which is the subject of the simulation, or acquire a methodological knowledge of the process;

- construct their own cognitive model of the theories behind the simulation and the process;
- experiment with alternative proposals, 'what if'; the computer model helps to form hypotheses, stimulates creativity and systematic thought, inter-disciplinary and 'lateral'thinking, and permits the students to obtain confirmation on each of their hypotheses;
- obtain confirmation of the hypotheses they have formed, which can be verified and repeated;
- systemise their experimentation: since forming hypotheses is relatively easy, 'adhocism' (Jencks, 1972) is discouraged;
- actively orientate their learning: students are motivated to define tasks and objectives and to follow them through, forming hypotheses and strategies, or rather giving themselves a method for formulating hypotheses; the outcomes can be verified within the simulation;
- reproduce aspects of a real context with which students are asked to investigate, with a mind to future professional practice.

EDUCATIVE EXPERIMENTATION

The SimTorino virtual laboratory, even though local and confined to a charette, shows what a promising methodology scenario simulation can be for students, for realising that urban design should follow an inclusive approach, necessary for concretising shared commitments into projects. The methodology has proved its value in motivating students to acquire first-hand experience of practices and methods they need in order to decipher the complexity of this scale and interpret it consistently in the various stages of the design. The simulation allowed each student to identify and check the defined requirements and indications quantified in the specific floor area ratio for each land use destination.

Within the Research Unit an important part of the work of the professors with the students was the interpretation of the context, that of the northern extension of the Turin metropolitan area (Fig. 3). During the interpretative and knowledge-acquiring stage, preceding simulation and designing, the work aimed at identifying the 'materials' that defined the specific nature of the northern area, in the widest accepted meanings of the word, involving history, geography, sociology, transport and quantity surveying. The students were asked to interpret the context from the viewpoint of changes over several decades and to study the dynamics of the Turin metropolitan area as a dialogue with the environment and context, and as a modification of the present context, which we consider the etymology of the word 'design'[3]. Among the factors considered were the interrelations between demography, especially the social structure, accessibility, seen as the relationship between the origin and the requirements of mobility, directions for the Plan, in the sense of expectations and intentions of the public administrations, and the real-estate market, in its complicated inter-dependency of supply and demand,of decisions on location and

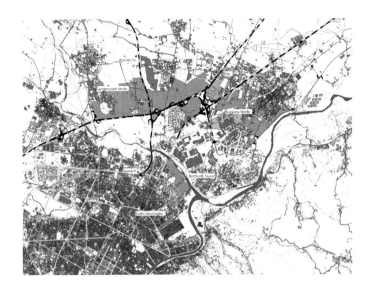

the expectations of investors and businesses. The analysis of each factor was peculiar to different disciplines: numerous experts participated in the virtual laboratory, and we recognise their contributions in the paragraph *Acknowledgements*.

Within the virtual laboratory a plurality of future scenarios for the northern urban area supported the students' designs in the exploration of the peculiarties of the context and environment. We decided to limit the combination between the various factors to just four scenarios; a number small enough for ease of interpretation yet which could open up a certain number of alternatives, especially if we consider that the single factors that are significant for each scenario can be inserted into a matrix and thus furnish additional permutations for future possibilities.

Scenario 1 assumes the construction of the projects in the Regulatory Plans and their Variants, leaving unchanged the existing town-planning systems, and foresees a new network accessibility with the adoption of an integrated Metropolitan Railway System, now being studied and planned in unison by the various Municipalities (Fig. 4).

Scenario 2, like the first, assumes the construction of the projects in the Regulatory Plans, but makes no changes to the transportation infrastructures and thus to the accessibility (Fig. 5).

Scenario 3 foresees the possible removal of the constraints on building construction and destination, leaving the extension and localisation (or re-localisation) of settlements to the mere market demand and supply, within the context of a new accessibility, created by an integrated Metropolitan Railway System (Fig. 6).

Scenario 4, like the third, leaves the extension and localisation of settlements to the mere market demand and supply, but makes no changes to the infrastructure and thus to the accessibility (Fig. 7).

The cognitive and descriptive contributions of our disciplines of architectural design and technology can be seen as fertile ground, yet they sometimes tend to be seen as indirect

3.
The northern extension of the Turin metropolitan area with the Variations approved to the Regulatory Plans.

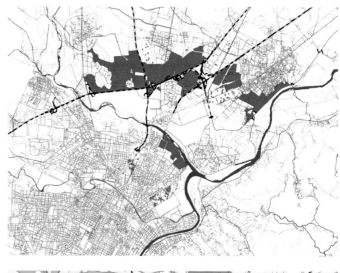

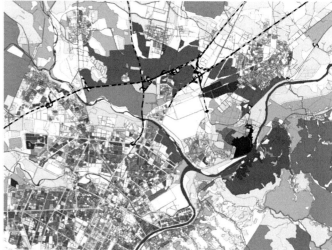

4.a-b
Scenario 1 results of the simulation to year 2026, map of the evolution of the built area and the location dynamics.

or secondary aspects in a project. We maintain that this critical situation depends on the role given to design in the construction of the city: "one can describe two basic models of the planner as a specialist in placemaking, within the context of urban planning, once certain objectives or general questions have been settled at the political level; one model presents the planner as the person who makes the decisions in the various disciplines involved in the planning and who transforms the results into a plan of physical placemaking; the other model puts the planner-designer on the same level as the other specialists, assigning to her/him proper conclusions to be offered in the inter-disciplinary structure which is brought about by successive approximations and assessments contributed by each specialist to all the material. What we find interesting for us is that among these contributions (which are also objectives, even if alternatives, in the various disciplines) there must appear, from the outset, the problem of the significance

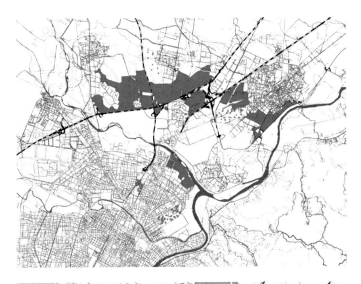

of the city and the territory, and that this problem can be isolated and studied in relation to the appropriate objectives (of meaning, or precision, of a new perception of reality) and that the architect must come up with appropriate spatial models that he can compare with the other contributions, the other forces that make up the form of the city" (Gregotti, 1993).

We believe that the virtual laboratory succeeded in targeting the cognitive and descriptive aspects for the students (Figs. 8 and 9) as reference points in the carrying out of the design: interpretative hypotheses in the commitment towards form, conceived of as usable for a period longer than the present (Harvey, 1993). These 'technical'questions are examples of how virtual laboratories help in dealing with various types of problem, each with its own disciplinary rules, and to adjust them and arrange them according to the needs of the design.

The interpretations of these factors and dynamics go beyond the bare indications of the plan, and become directions

5.a-b
Scenario 2 results of the simulation to year 2026, map of the evolution of the built area and the location dynamics.

for research in design that point the students towards the study of interpretations according to definite pre-established organisations of urban spaces that are functionally complex, owing to a mixture of activities, and towards the possibility of innovation at the point where the layout of the site meets the density and the distributive and spatial organisation.

The didactic experience derived from the SimTorino virtual laboratory has given the students the possibility to examine and experiment with certain basic principles of urban design: above all conceiving the design in terms of environment and landscape, and not as an isolated object, and thus countering the common tendency among students to judge the value of their proposals on the plane of novelty of shape, often tending towards the unusual, towards a contrast with existing forms or the search for an individual style. Vice versa, the scenario, or rather the scenarios in the plural, where the design takes place and has its context, are the tools proposed

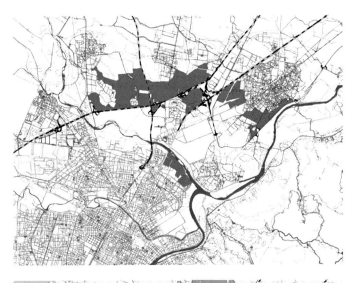

to set up a dialogue with the place and appraise the significance of a design over a longer period.

THE NOVEL CONTRIBUTIONS OF THE RESEARCH TO EDUCATION

To conclude, evaluating the work of the research gives us the opportunity to examine the contribution of simulation of scenarios to the teaching of urban design, where the experimentation has demonstrated the capability of:

- showing the relationship between activities, settlements and mobility. This is especially relevant for the city, in direct opposition to individualistic and particularising principles and follows an independent fragmentary method that loses sight of the complex nature of the urban design;
- participating in the inter-disciplinary approach that prioritises the integration of planning and design, overriding ad-

7.a-b
Scenario 4 results of the simulation to year 2026, map of the evolution of the built area and the location dynamics.

ministrative or disciplinary restrictions. Encouraging a more active relationship between different design phases, opening up to multi-disciplinary skills and intelligences, also originate in society. Promoting innovation in methodological tools and assuming a corresponding change in institutional instruments that are able to accept innovation in the practices, in a context that necessarily features conditions of uncertainty and plurality of actors and interests. As far as uncertainty is concerned, the educative experiments with the micro-simulation of design scenarios have shown how students can be plunged into the intricacies of urban governance, and can discover the degrees of uncertainty involved in the designs and programmes over a medium time span. In this way, the students can experience the educative limitations of the approach which seeks optimal solutions in a purely formal way, and at the same time they are introduced into the complexity of the design activity, which has to be able to deal with a wide range of interests, and should be able to avoid practices reductively responsive to different stimuli in a case-by-case approach, according to a practice of pure incrementalism. As far as regards plurality, the micro-simulation model allows the students to experiment at the urban scale with the real effects of complexity theory, according to which the dynamics of a system *emerges* from the non-linear interactions of the decisions of the individuals, even when conflicting, since they are subjectively legitimate and justified. In the simulations the decisions are made by families, workers, institutions and businesses, considered both individually and in groups. SimTorino allows the future architects to experiment with the simulation of the dynamics of the urban system as the *emergence* of the dynamics of location, transport and environment, by means of interaction between a) the location decisions of the individuals (families, businesses, workers), b) the subsequent dynamics in land– and building-use, and real estate values, c) the policies of the public decision-makers towards the creation of infrastructures, facilities and projects, as well as planning and regulations. In this way, the students have dealt with the real effect of theories of *emergence* and self-organisation of urban phenomena (Batty, 2005), enabling them at the same time to face the challenges and the opportunities for urban and regional design;

- experimenting with a new approach to urban design. The innovation core is in designing scenarios that take into account the wide range of possible dynamics in the metropolitan system, as an expression and representation of the multiplicity of powers and interests (simulated, obviously), as an evaluation of the design and planning alternatives in the wide range of the scenarios, and as a method and tool for dealing with multiplicity by means of the analysis and highlighting of decisional and strategic trajectories.

- evaluate the simulation by scenarios as a promising tool for making students aware of urban design as an inclusive tool, indispensible for translating shared aims into projects and designs. The tool has shown itself essential for gaining first-hand experience of the practices and methods necessary to understand the complexities that are a feature of urban design, and to interpret them according to the various phases of a project. The simulation allowed each student to identify and verify the location and development demands, as well as the requirements themselves, quantified for each land-use. The interpretations of these territorial dynamics are no longer mere indications for planning, but instead become design directions, which involve the student in the search for interpretations, according to definite pre-established organisations of urban spaces that are functionally complex, with a mixture of activities and typologies and the possibility of innovation at the point where the layout of the site meets the density and the distributive and spatial organisation.

The virtual laboratory conducts a dialectics between design and scenarios as pre-figurative tools offered to the students. Scenarios in the sense of oriented towards possible, open, multiform futures that the students have to interpret figuratively at the urban scale. This figurativeness must be developed and defined in a dialogue with the other scales of the design, so as to exercise overall control of the crucial issues of the surroundings and the environment.

These are issues that have become so complex that any tool seems inadequate to deal with them. On balance, the experimentation of the tools and methods demonstrates their ability to confront students with a well-structured outline of urban issues. The research signals an advance towards a closer integration of pre-figuration and figurativeness, towards effective tools for dealing with the complexity of the themes, the landscape

and consequently the urban texture to which the project is designed to give form, by means of a greater and more detailed stratification of meanings and the relations between them.

ACKNOWLEDGEMENTS

SimTorino is the outcome of a multi-disciplinary research project set up by the High Quality Laboratory – Integrated Territorial Project of Politecnico di Torino. The team who contributed to the carrying out of the research consists of:
- implementation of the model: Francesco Guerra and Alfonso Montuori, Politecnico di Torino;
- creation of the database: Andrea Ballocca; the Province of Turin and CSI Piemonte, Francesco Guerra, Politecnico di Torino;
- Transport model: Francesco De Florio, Politecnico di Torino, Corrado Bason, Agency for Metropolitan Mobility;
- construction of scenarios: Liliana Bazzanella, Franco Corsico, Giuseppe Roccasalva, Politecnico di Torino;
- virtual reality: Elena Masala, Stefano Pensa, Politecnico di Torino.

The City of Turin, the Province of Turin, the ISI foundation for Scientific Exchange and the Agency for Metropolitan Mobility also contributed to the research in various ways.

9.a-b
Photos of the northern extension of the Turin metropolitan area.

NOTES

[1] "Is urban planning dead?", is the provocative question asked by Jane Jacobs in her book on American cities: Jane Jacobs, *Life and death in the great cities: an essay on American metropolises,* New York: Random House, 1961.

[2] *http: //www.laq-tip.polito.it/*

[3] From the Latin *projèctus, 'thrown forward'.*

BIBLIOGRAPHY

Batty, Michael. *Cities and complexity: understanding cities with cellular automata, agent-based models, and fractals.* Cambridge (MA): MIT Press, 2005.

Bazzanella, Liliana; Caneparo, Luca; Corsico, Franco; Roccasalva. Giuseppe. (eds.). *Future Cities and Regions. Simulation, Scenario and Visioning, Governance and Scales.* New York, Heidelberg: Springer, printing.

Boyd, Susan; Chan, Roy. *Placemaking tools for community action.* CONCERN, 2002.

Brail, Richard K. *Planning support systems for cities and regions.* Cambridge (MA): New Lincoln Institute, 2008.

Caneparo, Luca. "SimCity. La programmazione urbanistica tra reale e virtuale", in *Rassegna,* vol. 81; p. 110-121, 2005

Choay, Françoise. *L'urbanisme: utopies et réalités.* Paris: Ed. du Seuil, 1965.

Ciribini, Giuseppe. *Tecnologia e progetto: argomenti di cultura tecnologica della progettazione.* Turin: Celid, 1984.

Desportes, Marc. Picon, Antoine. *De l'espace au territoire: L'aménagement en France XVIe – XXe siècles.* Paris, Presses De L'ecole Nationale Des Ponts Et Chaussees. 1997.

Downs, Anthony. *New Visions for Metropolitan America.* Washington, DC: Brookings Institution Press, 1994.

Gabetti, Roberto. *Progettazione architettonica e ricerca tecnico-scientifica nella costruzione della città – Storia e progetto.* Milan: Franco Angeli, 1983.

Gregotti, Vittorio. *Il territorio dell'architettura.* Milan: Feltrinelli, 1993.

Hall, Peter. *Cities of tomorrow: an intellectual history of urban planning and design in the twentieth century.* Oxford: Basil Blackwell, 1988.

Harvey, David. *La crisi della modernità.* Milan: il Saggiatore, 1993.

Hopkins, Lewis D.; Zapata, Marisa A. *Engaging the Future: Forecasts, Scenarios, Plans, and Projects.* Cambridge (MA): New Lincoln Institute, 2007.

Husserl, Edmund. *Die Krisis der europäischen Wissenschaften und die transzendentale Phänomenologie: Eine Einleitung in die phänomenologische Philosophie.* Dordercht: Lancaster, 1961.

Jencks, Charles. Nathan, Silver. *Adhocism: The Case for Improvisation.* New York: Doubleday, 1972.

Kalay, Yehuda E. Jeong, Yongwook. "Collaborative Design Process Simulation Game", in *Connecting >> Crossroads of Digital Discourse.* Indianapolis: ACADIA, pp. 133-141, 2003.

Kwartler, Michael; Longo, Gianni. *Visioning and Visualization: People, Pixels, and Plans.* Cambridge (MA): New Lincoln Institute, 2008.

Lee, Douglass B. "Requiem for Large Scale Models", in *Journal of the American Planning Association,* 39, pp. 163-178, 1973.

Lurcott, Robert. *Regional Visioning Public Participation. Best Practices.* Sustainable Pittsburgh. 2005.

Myron, Orfield. *Metropolitics: A Regional Agenda for Community and Stability.* Washington, DC: Brookings Institution Press, 1998.

Savitch, H.V; Vogel, Ronald. "Paths to new regionalism", in *State and Local Government Review,* 12, pp. 158-168, 2000.

Schön, Donald. *Educating the Reflective Practitioner.* San Francisco: Jossey-Bass, 1987.

Waddell, Paul. Ševcíková, Hana. Socha, David. Miller, Eric. Nagel, Kai. "Opus: An Open Platform for Urban Simulation", in *London: Computers in Urban Planning and Urban Management Conference,* 2005.

Bridging the Distance. Recent Teaching Activities with Asian Universities

GUSTAVO AMBROSINI
LILIANA BAZZANELLA
MICHELE BONINO
PIERRE-ALAIN CROSET

There has been for some time a long tradition of in-group workshops, where students from different Schools work side by side. These usually tend, however, to be of short duration, with the work concentrated into a few days or weeks. Two occasions (one recent and the other still in progress) in which the Italian partner was the Politecnico di Torino, attempted to recreate the atmosphere of intense and fruitful dialogue typical of workshops, but also to extend them to the length and breadth of a semester-long design studio.

The first case was a Design Unit carried out in common between the I Faculty of Architecture of Politecnico di Torino and the School of Architecture of the Tsingshua University of Beijing, during the spring semester of the academic year 2007-2008; work on the Italian side was coordinated by Gustavo Ambrosini, Michele Bonino, and Pierre-Alain Croset[1]. Eight Italian and eight Chinese students worked together from January to June 2008, in mixed groups coordinated by teachers from both schools; the final deadline was to be the debate and exhibition organised for the XIII World Congress of Architects UIA in Turin (29 June-3 July 2008)[2]. The form of the collaboration had been previously worked out in detail: it began with a month-long preparatory stage carried out in each group's home base, followed by two weeks spent by the Italian students in Beijing (February 2008) to see the places involved in the project along with their Chinese colleagues. After this initial full-immersion stage, in which the groups were formed (each made up of two Italians and two Chinese) and the first scenarios drawn up, there followed three months of work at a distance: a monthly videoconference between students and teachers was used to exchange designs and opinions, but an important role was played by continual informal contacts between the students (e-mails, blogs, messenger, Skype) and between the teachers. In June the Chinese students and teachers arrived in Turin, to finalise the work and get ready for the Congress deadline.

The theme of the project was the re-use of the Beijing Olympics installations, which were about to appear on the world stage at the inauguration of the Games on August the 8th, 2008. Attention was given to four of the structures: the Olympic Park and the Water Cube; the Wukesong centre, used for basketball and baseball; the Stadium and Workers' Gymnasium; and the installation for rowing and canoeing at Sunyi, one of the satellite cities of Beijing. An idea of re-utilisation had emerged that was difficult to reconcile with physical notions like 'conservation' of 'substi-

tution' but was rather an idea of action that would address broader issues: what identity, for example, could be given to the public open space, in the relationship between new complexes and established lifestyles? How could the monumental nature of the huge sport complexes be interpreted in such a way as to assign to them new meanings after the Olympics? And how could environmental sustainability be promoted as the key strategy in the reutilisation of the new structures?

The second experiment in collaboration is still underway: a joint project between the I School of Architecture and the Konkuk University GSD of Seoul has been taking place every year between the two schools. The first was from March to July 2008, when the students from the two laboratories were joined by a group from the Alta Scuola Politecnica: the coordination on the Italian side was handled by Gustavo Ambrosini and Michele Bonino[3]. The second 'Joint Studio' took place the following academic year, from September to December 2008, coordinated by Liliana Bazzanella and Michele Bonino[4]. The two Design Units followed a similar schedule; in the first case, the work began with a visit to Konkuk University by the teachers from Turin in March 2008, to work out the theme with their Korean colleagues and explain it to the students. During a two-day workshop, repeated ten days later in Turin with the Italian students, work began on the Turin theme, which involved the large scale systematic organisation of an area to the north of the city near the confluence of the Stura and Po rivers. At the end of the teaching period, the Korean teachers and students travelled to Turin to present jointly the research results, also in this case at the XXIII World Congress of Architects UIA.

The following academic year, the theme shifted to Seoul; it concerned the local housing situation where apartments were sold from a 'catalogue' (as if they were cars, both in terms of marketing and advertising, with the same degree of standardisation and the offers of optionals). This is a feature of the Korean market which encourages resi-

1.
Seoul. The repetitiveness of the aparto which characterizes much of the metropolis.

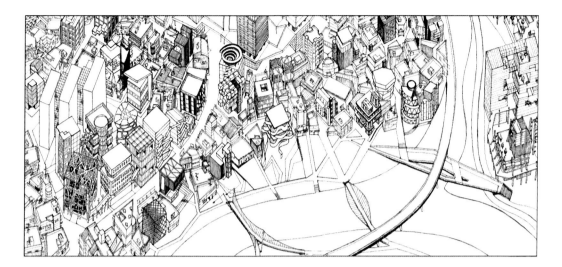

dential construction to be indifferent to urban relationships or social contexts, given the lack of concern as to where the housing modules on offer are located. In this case too, knowledge of the site and the theme was acquired in a two-day workshop in Turin, under the auspices of Konkuk University. The theme was then gradually developed through a series of exchanges on line or by videoconferences, until the final presentation which took place simultaneously in Seoul and Turin. A new Joint Studio with similar features was realized in the academic year 2009-2010, renewing the collaboration with Marco Bruno and his colleagues at Konkuk.

The way these Design Units were developed, despite the differences in interlocutors, places and methods, led us to some common reflections, mainly involving the difficulties and concerns created by distance: between topics and work methods, but also between customs and cultures. It appeared more educational to emphasise these distances, to give them critical form, rather than to strive for a harmonisation between models, a reconciliation that would probably have led to a uniformity of viewpoint and a globalisation of the images of the project[5]. We can discuss certain points of interest that emerged from the programme under the headings of three forms of 'distance'.

First distance: knowledge and sharing of the theme of the project

The recurrent question among the teachers in the initial stages of the Design Units was whether it was possible to operate consciously in places of which one could acquire a superficial direct knowledge or even merely indirect knowledge. This is certainly a clear break with a tradition in the teaching of architecture in Italy, where there has always been a regard for the place and attention paid to context, as keystones of the design experience. However, in the cases we have here, dis-

2.
View of an ideal Seoul made of bridges, aparto and bang designed by students of Turin during the exchange program between Polito and Konkuk. Authors of the drawings: Caterina Barioglio, Daniele Campobenedetto, Francesca Cavaleri, Giovanni Comoglio.

tance becomes an element with which precise teaching objectives can be built: working with the awareness of the differences and the distances of the phenomena, an awareness that can be acquired through an unambiguous process of reduction, which can stimulate the ability to synthesise and clarify the programme. At the same time, this reductive process can be seen as a way of measuring the danger of relying on western eyes which tend to see things according to biased certainties and apply a superficial exoticism. Deliberately accepting a reduction in the complexity of the problem helps to look at it with neutral and objective eyes, without clichés or prejudice.

The students showed a remarkable ability to take a critical view of contemporary urban dynamics of Asia, in some ways more 'at risk' since they are repeatedly depicted in a superficial manner in western reviews and publications, but their approach to the historical features of Beijing and Seoul was quite different. In many cases, the search for referents in the traditional cultures they came into contact with hovered between real understanding of the phenomena and a tendency to pinpoint only the usual more obvious aspects. A doubt often remained: that what we looked for in the other reality was actually already part of our imaginings. For example, in the Korean hanok the students often came across representations of figures of community life that were also part of modern western culture; in the historical Chinese gardens they found archetypes of nature mimicked by European culture; or even, in the other direction, in the classic forms of the Italian palazzo one could identify the symbols of authoritarian power. This intricate relationship with history was only broken in some longer and more detailed Master Theses that originated with the Project[6].

Second distance: communication and method

In situations where 'speed' is a feature, as for example in an intensive workshop, the ability to communicate and produce images assumes an important role; at best, this can arise from an abundant capacity to be concise on the part of the students, in other cases it can be seen as a short cut compared with more complex design processes. Similarly, while working at a distance for a length of time, there are faster and more concentrated contacts, such as videoconferences; here too, we have to think rationally about the effectiveness of the communication. The image becomes the absolute, imposing itself on reality to the extent of replacing it. Communicative codes are linked together by a large number of cross-references: to the 'reality' that is observed and encoded in the programme, but also to different images produced by 'high' culture. The main risk is that this will obliterate the perception of what is real, because of an ever more urgent superimposition of images and pictures that no longer replace a direct contact with the place and its problems. In an attempt to minimise this risk, both in Chinese and Korean workshops we decided to work simultaneously on two well-

3.a
Torino-Seoul Design Studio 1 (2007-2008). Workshop at Konkuk University, March 2008.

3.b
Torino-Seoul Design Studio 1 (2007-2008). The final presentation at the XXIII World Congress of Architecture UIA, July 2008.

defined levels: one more flexible level where the precision required in real contexts could be simplified by forming preparatory considerations that could also be applied directly to contacts at a distance; and a deeper level sustained throughout the length of the project where there was no need for frequent sharing but of continuous reflection. The final synthesis of these two channels progressing at different speeds led to very interesting results: in the Korean case, for example, a re-thinking of housing types that were at first considered to be 'aggressive' (high buildings, huge containers, etc.) in favour of replacing the urban fabric with more modest and less obvious forms of architecture, characterised by a module that could be reproduced in the density of the Korean city.

Other aspects were noted: for example, the great effectiveness of frequent informal contacts between the students (blogs, messengers, etc.) over and above the official channels of videoconferences or the more formal discussions via e-mail under the guidance of the teachers, from whom initially a large part of the results of the exchange was expected. One limitation in the case of the Korean collaboration has so far been a lack of feeling between the two groups of students, because in their case there has been no live contact between them, as was the case with the Beijing group. Another factor worth noting is the almost continuous working cycle thanks to the time difference which gave China and Korea an 'advantage' of 7 and 8 hours respectively[7].

Third distance: cultural exchange

As they worked on the themes proposed by the two Asian universities and which were located in the two cities, the Italian students (and teachers) often looked for references and reasons within the local culture on which to base the choices they made in the project.

It could be useful to look closer at how this worked. Obtaining clues from other cultures is often something that is 'directed' by the design problem we are dealing with, but also by our own personal researches and cognitive processes. It is a process that occurs over and over again in the history of architecture, as for example in the 18th century, when the forms and perceptions of the Chinese garden happily encountered the developing taste for the English version, and important innovations ensued. Many modern architects have read the features of other cultures in novel and purposeful ways: for Frank Lloyd Wright, the disintegration of the boundaries between interiors and exteriors and the proportions (tatami) of the traditional Japanese house; for Aldo van Eyck, the sense of identity and community in the spatial structure of Dogon villages. We could add many more examples to the list, but it is important to note that we are not looking only at traditions, but also at contemporary phenomena that affect our sensibilities. There could be a re-thinking of the traditional hutong type of housing that involved creating new models of contemporary form, both physically and socially, in which a response could be sought

4.a
Torino-Beijing Design Studio 2008.
The first revision at Tsinghua
University, February 2008.

4.b
Torino-Beijing Design Studio 2008.
The final presentation at the XXIII
World Congress of Architecture UIA,
June 2008.

to the (western) idea of neighbourhood units. In the same way, the're-interpretation' of the multi-use buildings typical of modern Seoul, where multi-storey shops, offices and other social spaces co-exist together, can be seen as the realisation of a (western) idea of hybridisation.

The mental process of 'understanding the other' that is developed during an applied research such as a designing experience, is thus never a neutral process but instead one that creatively weaves together the filters and intellectual anxieties of our culture. It is a process in which the emancipating search for what is, or appears to be, new, can take us down paths we have already travelled, to end up as a way of reformulating a problem that already derives from our searching, finding answers for ourselves through a form of 'lateral thinking' which tackles the issues from a different point of view altogether.

If this turns out to be the most common cause of contamination, we can better understand the apparent differences in approach that often emerged between the western and eastern students, and which led often to confrontation: the western student was seen to be generally more curious about the local culture than the oriental student, who was often more attracted to what we would describe as a globalising internationalism, but which they saw as a characteristic 'sign' of western design culture.

An example of this attitude was the relationship of the Italian and Chinese students regarding the redevelopment of the Olympic structures: the Italians saw this theme as a chance to obtain design tools that were bound up with ancient oriental cultural values, such as the preoccupation with nature, the central position given to the human form, and communal life; the Chinese, even though they proved to be excellent 'tutors' on these subjects, gave priority to the image and the visibility of landmarks, seeing in them the origins of the most spectacular and iconic products of contemporary western designers.

5.a
Torino-Seoul Design Studio 2 (2008-2009). The present apartment buildings in Seoul.

A SEMANTIC ANALYSIS OF DISTANCE INTERACTIONS IN THE PROJECT UNIT

LUCA CANEPARO

In order to gain some clear introductory ideas on the methods of distance communication in the design workshops, and to analyse and study the amount of distance collaboration between teachers and students, we experimented with a method of semanticising the multimedia materials that were collected during the course of the Project. The method consists in the defining of certain semantic levels, categorising them, analysing any semantically similar elements in the material and finally creating a proper semanticisation of the multimedia materials.

Semanticisation is a process that is closely linked to the context and culture where it takes place, and it is not intended or employed to replace cognitive methods nor reduce distances, but rather to suggest, for innovative experimentation, methods for describing any complexities and translating their meanings into the terms of the project. The semantic representation scheme adopted by our research belongs to the field of computer science and specifically to that of artificial intelligence, which can supply the tools for associating symbols with multimedia units.

Our research began by freeing the field from any unrealistic attempts at objectivising or organising representations on the levels of meaning; levels, in the plural, since semantic representations cannot be and were not intended to be unambiguous. The innovation lies in the flexibility and simplicity of defining semantic units using natural language. As such, it can be 'automatically' translated in ways whereby the remote interactions of the design projects can be analysed and studied, and the cause and effects of the distances under consideration.

Some examples of semantic structuring and categorisation are shown below.

Putting the method into practice was not only simplified but actually made possible by non-linear semantic montage software written by Professor Vincenzo Lombardo of the Information Science and MultiDAMS Department of the University of Turin.

Purely for the purpose of illustrating the method and the tool, rather than of their results, which are still awaited, segments of video are accessible on the web, automatically generated by the semantic montage software. They are examples of the numerous, if not countless, videos that the system can generate based on the choices teachers and students can make on the semantic level, by highlighting the semantic categories that are of interest to them. The software automatically generates a video by assembling the multimedia units that are semantically closest to the categories wanted by the user[8].

These video examples are based on experiments on the semanticisation of multimedia units, oriented according to three levels or classes, respectively:

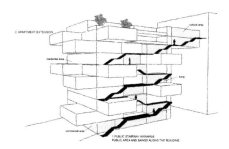

1. Architecture
2. Design
3. Communicative/collaborative process

For each of these classes values (also known as sub-classes) were defined, for example:

For Architecture
• public open space
• monumentality
• environmental sustainability

For Design
• knowledge
• investigation
• work
• finishing

For Communicative/collaborative process
• task management
• team working
• decision making

We can continue the subdivisions, in the sense that 'open public space' can include within it further sub-classes and so on…

Some classes can be structured temporally, for example the sub-classes of Design could include a chronological sequencing of the activities carried out on the Project.

On the subject of classes and classifications, Borges, in the Analytic language of John Wilkins, quoting from an imaginary Chinese encyclopaedia, declared that "animals can be divided into the following classes: a) those belonging to the emperor, b) those that are embalmed, c) those that have been tamed, d) suckling pigs, e) mermaids, f) fabulous beasts, g) stray dogs, h) those included in this classification, i) those that end up mad, j) countless others, k) those painted with a fine camel-hair brush, l) etcetera, m) those who have just broken the jug, n) those that from a distance look like flies".

Every classification is arbitrary (and risky); so the semantications used should be considered only for the purpose of documenting the postulates of a method, above all its aptitude for defining structure and classes in order to form and prove conjectures on meaning in terms of distance interaction on the topics of the research project.

6.a
Torino-Seoul Design Studio 2 (2008-2009). The project of student Miriam Bozzuto.

6.b
Torino-Seoul Design Studio 2 (2008-2009). A videoconference between Politecnico di Torino Politecnico di Torino and Konkuk University (LAQ-TIP, Turin).

NOTES

[1] The idea originated in the communal participation of the two schools in the 2006 Venice Biennale (workshop "Learning from cities", run by Francesco Garofalo) and in the subsequent contacts between deans Carlo Olmo and Zhu Wenyi.

[2] Beijing-Torino Design Studio 2008. OLYMPEKed: a study on Beijing 2008 Olympic Venues Redevelopment. Tsinghua University – School of Architecture; Politecnico di Torino – I School of Architecture. Partner: Beijing Planning Bureau. Academic Year. 2007-2008. Teachers: Zhu Wenyi, Liu Jian, Zhang Li, Zhu Yufan (Tsinghua University), Gustavo Ambrosini, Michele Bonino, Pierre-Alain Croset (Politecnico di Torino). Students: Shang Qian, Yang Yang, Guo Yong, Xie Yingying, Sun Pengui, Chen Xiaoji, Fu Siliang, Li Hongyuan (Tsinghua University), Francesca Diano, Marta Fantini, Fabrizio Fregoni, Roberto Garcia Leone, Alberto Lessan, Manuele Mandrile, Mariana Michalcikova, Claudio Sframeli (Politecnico di Torino). Final presentation of the Projects: Officine Grandi Riparazioni, Turin, 29 June 2008, at 11.30, con the participation of Lucio Barbera (Sapienza Università di Roma), Paolo Bellino (Torino Olympic Park), Carlo Olmo (Politecnico di Torino), Carlos Sambricio (ETSA Madrid), Ferruccio Zorzi (Politecnico di Torino). Exhibition: Castello del Valentino, room 9, 30 June – 5 July 2008 (official off-congress event of the XXIII World Congress of Architecture UIA). Catalogue: OLYMPEKed, Tsinghua University Press, Beijing, printing.

[3] Turin-Seoul Design Unit, Academic Year 2007-2008. Tutors: Marco Bruno, Sang Hun Lee, Christiane Wunderlich (Konkuk University), Gustavo Ambrosini, Paolo Napoli (Politecnico di Torino), Michele Bonino, Pierre-Alain Croset, Paolo Pileri (Alta Scuola Politecnica). Around 44 Korean and Italian students were involved overall in the Design Unit. Final presentation of the Projects: Officine Grandi Riparazioni, Turin, 2 July 2008 (official off-congress event of the XXIII World Congress of Architecture UIA), with the participation of Francesca Camorali (Urban Center Metropolitano), Ippolito Ostellino (Parco del Po Tratto Torinese), Paolo Verri (Comitato Italia 150).

[4] Turin-Seoul Design Unit, Academic Year 2008-2009. Tutors: Marco Bruno, Choon Choi (Konkuk University), Liliana Bazzanella, Michele Bonino con Alberto Bologna, Cristiano Picco (Politecnico di Torino). Around 49 Korean and Italian students were involved overall in the Design Unit. Final presentation of the Projects: Turin and Seoul, 16 and 17 December 2008, with the participation of Monica Antinori (Fondazione Promozione Acciaio), Tomà Berlanda (Politecnico di Torino), Andrea Boschetti (Metrogramma), Luca Molinari (Naples University, Aversa,) in Turin. The combined Design Unit planned for the Academic Year 2009-2010 will be organised along similar lines. The theme will change, however, and will concentrate on the topic of buildings for commercial use in South Korea, particular attention being paid to high-density urban textures.

[5] 'Distance' appears as a basic critical category in reflections on 'knowledge' in Carlo Ginzburg, Occhiacci di legno. Nove riflessioni sulla distanza, Feltrinelli, Milan 1998. "I have understood better...that familiarity, which in the final analysis is linked to culture, cannot be an important criterion. 'The whole world is one country' (a well known italian proverb) does not mean that everything is the same: it means that all of us are out of our element with regard to something or someone." Preface, ibid., p.

[6] See for example Marta Fantini, OlympekED. Beijing-Torino Design Studio 2008. Progetto per un parco urbano a Pechino, degree thesis 13 July 2009, supervisor P.-A. Croset, assistant supervisors G. Ambrosini and M. Bonino: a contemporary interpretation of the hutong texture and the relative public spaces.

[7] + 6 e + 7 hours in the case of European Summer Time.

[8] For example http://frigo.polito.it: 8080/grid/temp/Beijing-Torino_design_studio.av

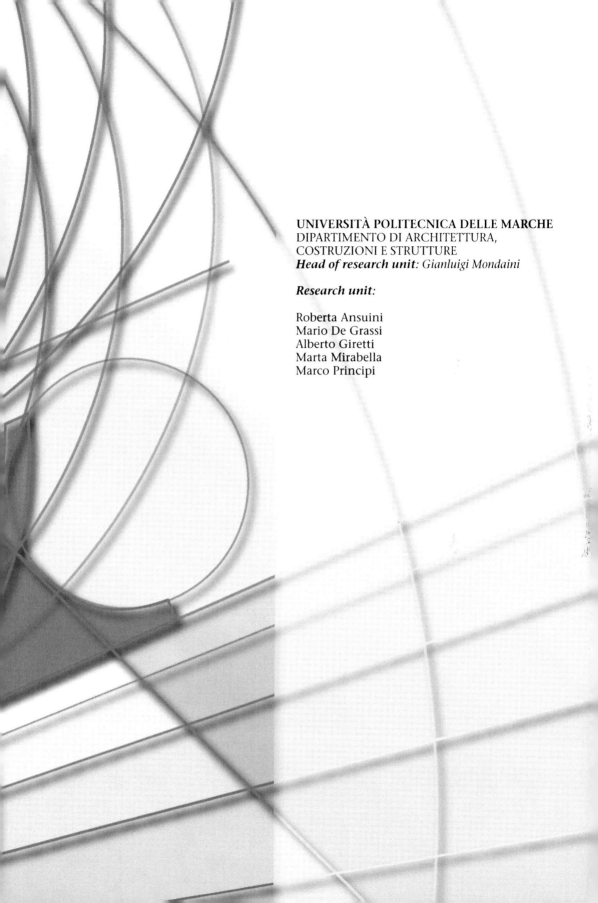

UNIVERSITÀ POLITECNICA DELLE MARCHE
DIPARTIMENTO DI ARCHITETTURA,
COSTRUZIONI E STRUTTURE
Head of research unit*: Gianluigi Mondaini*

Research unit:

Roberta Ansuini
Mario De Grassi
Alberto Giretti
Marta Mirabella
Marco Principi

Functional and semantic characterization of multimedia and interactive course supported by conceptual database

Gianluigi Mondaini
Alberto Giretti
Mario De Grassi
Roberta Ansuini

As partner in the "Research and experimental evaluation of e-learning new model and technologies in architecture education", the research unit of Università Politecnica delle Marche worked on the identification of a realistic approach to e-learning in architecture, through the functional and semantic characterization of multimedia and interactive course supported by conceptual database. We speak of "realistic approach" because experimental research work carried on in the last years in our group highlighted that the perception of the learning model offered by the teachers and recieved by the students are coming apart, in terms of completeness, effectiveness and efficiency.

First of all this situation is due to the fact that Architectural Design is notoriously known to be a difficult teaching field, in which the cognitive activities are more complex and the cultural and academic controversies are almost infinite. So, there is a complexity in the architectural design education domain that make more arduous the "e-learning translation", because this domain is feature by the usage of not fully shared models and methods.

Altough, there is an other factor, that emerged in many cases, that consists in the lack of specifici model and tools for e-learning in architecture education.

Learning to design is not only a question of practise. Design is one of the most complex types of problem solving tasks involving cultural, cognitive and technological aspects. So it follows that teaching design is not only a question of experience.

In this context our research unit worked in order to define cognitive requirements for the development of e-learning corse in Architectural Design.

Traditionally, the practice of Architecture, Engineering and Construction (A/E/C) design is learned through a design studio approach. In order for design assistance activities to be as efficient as possible, the cognitive processes characterizing this type of problem solving must be known as clearly as possible – this applies to the knowledge of how the processes themselves are communicated and transmitted. Hence, what is needed is precise knowledge of design as a complex process where a multitude of aspects and perspectives converge. Comprehension of design processes is indispensable in view of every type of modelling activity which has to deal with design learning courses, be it web based or traditional. We experimentally analysed via protocol analysis the learning processes typical of design and related knowledge.

Understanding the design "phenomenon" requires the assumption of a set of models which can effectively guide the observation procedure. After a recognition of the main design models in the literature, they have been applied operatively in real design learning environments (academic courses), that have been analysed, with the help of videotaping and protocols.

Based on these analysis, traditional learning and e-learning have been compared and main critical states identified. Finally requirements for e-learning course in architectural design have been defined.

1. CURRENT TRENDS IN DESIGN COGNITION RESEARCH

The problem of design has acquired, over the course of time, increasing importance because it, in fact, makes up the activity that qualifies and regulates economic, social, and environmental impact, the quality of life, and technological development in contemporary society. During the last 20 years, design has had the opportunity, like never before, to take advantage of highly sophisticated and powerful instruments in the field of information technology. New instruments have rapidly transformed the design process and, at the same time, have had a powerful stimulus for innovation thanks to it. However, in many academic fields the opinion, of idealistic origin, that design cannot be discussed in a technical, objective sense because it is an eminently artistic-creativ activity, and hence, connected to mysterious recesses of intuition, it is still very common. If the phenomenal contributions subsequently lightened up the initial drastic theoretic closure, even today, "the major part of the literature regarding the manner in which designers design is left up to anecdotes or personal introspective and has never led to any reproducible results" [Gero, 1998].

Recent studies in the field of cognitive science aim at overcoming the popular character, which up to nowadays, the theme of describing the design activity has been fixed and the cognitive processes more generally through a strict validation carried out using scientific analysis of the processes in course. The discipline, known as Design Studies promotes the rapidly emerging scientific study of design in the international community – terms of man's qualified activity. In 1984 Cross edited a series of papers presenting a history of the Developments in design methodology, collecting texts written by researchers who had been involved in the underlying "movement" [Cross, 2004]. The collection covers the period that goes from 1962 to 1982 and reflects the progression of the movement through four stages:

- prescription of an ideal design process: the period of systematic design" proposed by the proponents of the "design methods movement";
- description of the intrinsic nature of design activity: design problems were discovered to be not so amenable to systematization; authors tried to understand their apparent complexity, attributing it in large part to design problems' "ill-structured ness";
- observation of the reality of design activity: methodical collection of data on the actual design activity;

- reflection on the fundamental concepts of design: emergence of a more fundamental and philosophical approach to design method.

Today, these lines of reflection are still present, and we can summarize the current trends of design research according to three main guidelines:

- a theoretical view, concerned with the study of the nature of design, aiming at deriving an abstract theory of design, which can be applied for the improvements of actual design processes, as well as to the construction of supporting systems.
- an operational view concerned with the representation of the design procedures, the identification of its phases, and the rationalization of the interaction among the many participating figures
- a cognitive view concerned with the analysis and modeling of design process conceived as the outcome of a special human cognitive activity, that of designing.

1.1. Theoretical Models of Design

The origins of the theoretical modeling of the design process can be traced to the early studies by Alexander, Simon and Rittel and in particular to Simon's work "The Science of the Artificial" [Simon, H. A., 1999]. He first argued that designing can be taught, learnt and practiced in a systematic way; and first introduced a characteristic of design problems nowadays considered one of its main specificities: their "ill-structured" character. According to Simon, "ill-structured" problems lack:

- a definite criterion for testing any proposed solution, usually the vague concept of "satisfying" (i.e. finding an acceptable solution rather than calculating the best solution amongst all the possibilities) is the only evaluation criteria;
- one or more problem spaces where the initial problem state, the goal state, and all other, intermediary states that may be reached, or considered, can be represented in the course of attempting a solution to the problem;
- one or more problem spaces where any knowledge that the problem solver can acquire about the problem can be represented;
- a possibility to define, with complete accuracy, the changes in the world that the design may bring about.

Simon does not consider "ill-structured ness" or "well-structured ness" an absolute characteristic. The boundary between well-structured and ill-structured problems is vague, fluid and not susceptible to formalization. In some sense, designing is the art of structuring problems. Once the problem structure has been defined, the solution is ready made. Reasoning on the design of a house, Simon argues that even such a "typically ill-structured" problem rapidly acquires structure, attributable to the fact that the designer applies certain strategies, such as decomposition: "During any given short period of time, the architect will find himself working on a problem which, perhaps beginning in an ill-structured state, soon converts itself through evocation from memory into a well-structured problem". Thus, for Simon, design problems may seem ill structured at first sight, but the designer rapidly structures them and then solves the well-structured problem version.

In theoretical models, the central defining characteristic of the design activity is its problem solving nature, which in turn, is essentially a symbolic information processing task. An ill-structured global problem, such as the design of a house, is rather smoothly amenable to a set of well-structured sub-problems. Solving ill-structured design problems proceeds through two consecutive stages:

- first structuring the ill-structured problem,
- then solving the resulting well-structured problem or problems.

Simon's remarks that: "There is merit to the claim that much problem solving effort is directed at structuring problems, and only a fraction of it at solving problems once they are structured" [Simon, 1973/1984]. If one realizes how much time in product-development projects, is spent in design — and especially in the early "conceptual design" stages, i.e. the core design activity from a cognitive viewpoint, this "structuring" activity is then perhaps what characterizes these early development stages. Solving an ill-structured problem requires the formulation of goals, as do all goal-oriented activities, such as problem solving. Even if the goals of an ill-structured problem are imprecise, they necessarily rely on criteria, which the person already disposes of, be it implicitly. From the pioneering works, a number of global descriptive models of actual design have been developed.

Proposals for design models generally focus on particular aspects of the design process. Darses [Darses, 1990] has formulated elements for a model of design based on constraint management, focusing on solution generation. Case based design [Schreiber et al, 1994] introduces a memory based process for the structuring of problem space and solution findings, CommonKADS [Maher, 1995] focuses on the formalization of the knowledge involved in the design process, model-based design [Bhatta and Goel, 1994] extends the design problem space with the explicit representation of the physical behaviour of devices and components.

1.2 Operational Models of Design

Operational models of design are developed in order to plan and monitor the design process. Operational models are built combining two lines of representation. On one side, they stipulate that problem solving follows an abstract – concrete axis (going from conceptual to physical specifications) by an iteration of two complementary stages: generation of a solution (that may be partial or intermediate) and its evaluation, which leads to the generation of a better solution, which itself is evaluated, and so on until the ultimate solution is obtained. On the other side, design is represented as a series of phases to be followed in a top-down, stepwise manner [Blessing, 1994]. A design stage has been defined as a "subdivision of the design process based on the state of the product under development". In each stage, varieties of techniques appropriate to the main task are proposed. Stages may be decomposed into finer stages, which may correspond to "activities". Several operational models do not merely cover the design process, but the artefact's global lifecycle, from the "policy stage", passing through the macro-stage of "design", to the use or disposal of the product.

In the engineering design domain, many operational design models have been proposed. A famous example and reference in mechanical engineering, is the prescriptive four-stage model by Pahl and Beitz [Pahl and Beitz, 1996]:
- analysis (i.e. product planning);
- conceptual design;
- embodiment design (i.e. draft design);
- Detail design.

Other authors add as fifth and sixth stages:
- evaluation and decision taking;
- Presentation of results.

Another reference in the engineering design literature is the ASE paradigm, which distinguishes three stages, i.e. analysis, synthesis, evaluation. The three-stage ASE framework constitutes the basis of the "systematic design" method and has been widely accepted in the design methodology community.

1.3. Cognitive Models of Design

Simon states that "design" is not restricted to architects and engineers: "They are not the only professional designers. Everyone who devises courses of action aimed at changing existing situations into preferred ones designs. The intellectual activity that produces material artefacts is not fundamentally different from the one that prescribes remedies for a sick patient, the one that devises a new sales plan for a company or a social welfare policy for a state" [Simon, 1999]. Engineering, medicine, business, education, law, architecture, and painting are "all centrally concerned with the process of design". Nowadays, the view that design is a type of cognitive activity, not a professional status restricted to certain professionals, called "designers", is widely accepted. Cognitive research on design is focused on understanding the kinds of human reasoning that are involved in design and the human cognitive resources involved in such processes.

The beginning of the cognitive research on design modeling can be traced back to Schön's proposal of the reflective-practice concept. Schön's research was concerned with the way in which "professionals think in action" as "reflective practitioners", and the consequent education of such reflective practitioners [Schön, 1983]. Schön considers "designing reflective conversation with the materials of a design situation", where the practitioner's effort to solve the reframed problem yields new discoveries which call for new reflection-in-action. The process spirals through stages of appreciation, action, and re-appreciation. Schon's concept of "knowledge in action" [Schön, 1992] states that making usually involves a number of competences very often not explicitly described by the actor, that is, they are the outcome of a reflective, almost unconscious stimulus. This involves the capacity of doing the right thing when in situ…exhibiting what we know mainly in what we do and by the way in which we do it.

Schon's work was one of the milestones of what is now called "Situated Cognition". A complementary approach grounded on the traditional view of cognitive psychology, uses the computational metaphor as a mean for describing and explaining human cognitive capacities. This approach shares a great deal with theoretical models, and inherits their concepts, the vocabulary and a number of results.

Structured observations of design behaviour [Cross, 2004] showed that designers appear to be 'ill-behaved' problem solvers, especially in terms of the time and attention they spend on defining the problem. It appears that successful design behaviour is based not on extensive problem analysis, but on adequate 'problem scoping' and on a focused or directed approach to gathering problem information and prioritizing criteria. Processes of structuring and formulating the problem are frequently identified as key features of design expertise. The concept of 'problem framing' seems to capture the nature of this activity best. Successful, experienced and, especially, outstanding designers are found in various studies to be proactive in problem framing, actively imposing their view of the problem and directing the search for solution conjectures. A very special role in the problem framing process is played by the experience that has been modeled as a problem oriented organization of design cases often called precedents [Oxman Rivka, 1994]. Experience in a specific problem domain enables designers to move quickly identifying a problem frame and proposing a solution conjecture. Lloyd and Scott [Lloyd and Scott, 1994], from protocol studies of experienced engineering designers, found that solution-focused approach appeared to be related to the degree and type of previous experience of the designers. They found that more experienced designers used more 'generative' reasoning, in contrast to the deductive reasoning employed more by less-experienced designers. In particular, designers with specific experience of the problem type tended to approach the design task through solution conjectures, rather than through problem analysis. They concluded that 'It is the variable of specific experience of the problem type that enables designers to adopt a conjectural approach to designing, that of framing or perceiving design problems in terms of relevant solutions.' Furthermore, in some studies it has been noticed that creative, productive design behaviour seems to be associated with a frequent switching of cognitive activity types. There is no clear explanation for this observation, but it may be related to the need to make rapid explorations of problem and solution in tandem, in the co-evolution of problem and solution.

An other reference figure in the research regarding cognitive design is, with no a doubt, John Gero of Key Center of Design Computing at the University of Sidney. Gero is an architect and researcher who played an important, investigative role in the domain of "Artificial Intelligence in Design" [Gero, 1990-1998].

Gero's research started developing his so-called "function-behaviour-structure" model. The knowledge based design view let him distinguish among three models of designing:

Designing as search – The basic and often implicit assumption in designing as search is that the state space of possible designs is defined a priori and is bound. The designing processes focus on means of traversing this state space to locate either an appropriate or the most appropriate solution (depending on how the problem is formulated). The assumption that the space is defined a priori to searching relegates this model to detail or routine designing.

Designing as planning – Action planning is a well-known goal driven by the reasoning paradigm of Artificial Intelligence. From a theoretical point of view, action planning can be related to the searching.

Designing as exploration – It takes the viewpoint that the state space of possible designs to be searched is not necessarily available at the design process outset. Exploration may be viewed in two ways. It may be viewed as a form of meta-search: the designer searches for state spaces among the set of possible predefined state spaces. It may be viewed as a form of construction where each new state space bears some connection to the previously constructed state space (s). "Exploration connects with the ideas of conceptual or non-routine designing" [Logan and Smithers, 1993].

According to Gero's recent view, these three types of models do not adequately model design. In addition to the references to Schön's "reflection in action", he is now approaching 'situativity' notions, analyzing, e.g., "conceptual designing as a sequence of situated acts".

2. DESIGN LEARNING

One of the specific qualities of education in A/E/C is the central role played by the design process. In fact, education in A/E/C is principally directed to the instruction of designers; professionals capable of conceiving, constructing and renewing buildings, while satisfying specific requirements within a set of constraints. Therefore, the most important distinction between design instruction and practice, and instruction and practice in traditional academic disciplines, is that students are directed to a corpus of desirable outcomes rather than to principles or theories. Curricula for A/E/C Designers is deeply characterized by these specific traits:

* they involve a vast number of multi-faced competences, ranging from the humanistic field, such as the story of architecture, to skills that involve technology, such as thermal and acoustic design;
* the main cognitive and pedagogical references are largely that of constructivism, (Novak's meaningful learning [Novak, 1977], Schank's Goal Based Scenarios [Schank, 1992], Reflective Practitioner [Schön, 1983], learning by doing [Novak et al, 1984], etc...)
* classroom lessons are mainly directed to foster the constant interplay of theory and practice (there is a great deal in the way of discovering how principles affect the solution to a specific problem and how specific solutions may illustrate larger principles – fig. 1).

1.a-b-c
Classroom lesson in architectural design – typical phases.

Traditionally, the practice of architectural design is learnt through a design studio approach (fig. 2). In the studio, designers express and explore ideas, generate and evaluate alternatives, and lastly, they make decisions and take actions. They make external representations (drawings and three-dimensional models) and reason with these representations in order to inquire, analyze, and test hypotheses about the designs they represent.

In current academic courses, design studio education is reflected in homework revision practice. Students and teachers collaboratively develop a design theme; they share objectives, ideas, issues and solutions. Students' reflective practicing is continuously matched against the teacher's expertise, establishing a privileged way of expertise transfer.

During homework revision session communication teachers and students occurs via verbal communication but also (perhaps mainly) via other forms of expression and representation: gesture, sketches, and all kinds of visual and graphic Medias.

In our research various academic courses have been observed and analysed, in order to thoroughly investigate how Design Learning occurs in real learning environments. This was achieved by using mainly the two following methodologies:

- protocol analysis; that is, a technique which allows a parallel and correlated observation of the various kind of communication mains
- work in progress material collection; which allows summarizing the design process in phases.

2.1 Methodologies for Design Learning Practice Analysis

2.1.1 Protocol Analysis tool

This stage of the research aimed at understanding how the actual reality of Design Instruction can be referred to reference tutoring discourse frames and cognitive models of Design, in order to map the needs and the procedures of teaching/learning Architecture more thoroughly and give clues to define an appropriate Learning Design Model more clearly.

An extensive protocol analysis was performed on a set of design revision sessions in regular courses of Architecture-Engineering Degree at the Università Politecnica delle Marche (Italy). It involved two teachers and a number of student groups. The research was conducted adopting the following methodology:

- Observation and videotaping of student/teacher exchanges while reviewing design homework.
- Protocol analysis of videotapes according to the representation models of design and interaction and negotiation of meaning [De Grassi, 2005].

Semi-structured interviews of students and tutors in order to triangulate the observation and analyze data from more than one perspective and increase its reliability.

2.a-b
Students involved in a design studio: a) a homework revision session, b) students building a scale model of their design.

Protocol analysis is a data acquisition technique for eliciting highly detailed information regarding a particular process and is usually applied at the sub-process level. This method [Newell 1966, Ericsson e Simon 1993] is based on the transcription of the verbal content produced by the designer by applying the "thinking aloud" method (already part of teacher/student revision) and, on the subsequent process, subdividing the cognitive actions microscopically (micro-strategies) into sequences that generally last a few seconds, localized in the field of a precise semantic area.

The segments that appear more relevant (relative to remind processes or ideation processes) are isolated and codified and then subjected to a synthetic interpretation. Subsequently, an attempt is made to reconstruct a mnemonic model of the procedure used during the process in relation to different themes and the phases of the project's development.

The reconstruction of the cognitive process traces is also carried out through the significance obtained via a careful examination of the graphic component produced by the designer: sketches and drawings.

In this way, Protocol Analysis allows submitting transcripts and similar written records of a Design Process to systematic examination. It is certainly a time consuming method but given the field we are investigating it is also the most reliable way to highlight processes and critical areas, seeing as it also offers the possibility of analyzing discourse in action. The main focus of this technique is to get insights into the processes rather than the products. Its biases have been acknowledged by the scientific community but it still remains somewhere in the middle ground between "hard" empirical methods and "weak" purely observational methods.

We have thus video-recorded two subsequent revision sessions for three groups of students, lasting approx 20min each, transcribed the script and segmented it. The coding scheme was developed and the segments categorized accordingly. The coding scheme obviously corresponds to the framework of research that we projected on to the data and the coded categories are:

Design Cognition Process

Macro-Strategies	Multimodal perceptual design reasoning (conceptual level, perceptual level and external world)
Micro-Strategies	Proposing a Solution (proposing, clarifying, retracting, making a design decision, consulting external information, postponing a design action) Analyzing Solution (analyzing, justifying, evaluating)
Gesture and Sketches	Furthermore the verbal development, the non verbal communication flux is considered,

that includes gestures and visual
components, made clear through
reference images and graphical
signs (sketches)

Tutorial Discourse

Turns   time for students and tutor
Acts   according to the tutoring frame
Discourse Stategies   empathy, pauses, silence, fillers, etc.)

Our scheme of discourse analysis is clearly at a high level,
since it's been acknowledged that performing a finer level of
granularity on large data sets is particularly difficult. It aims at
identifying patterns on intentional acts (speech acts or movements), exchange structures (turn-taking patterns) and dialogue strategies. Such an analysis wants to reveal the roles participants take, the overall structure of the dialogue and the extent to which participants engage with each other's contribution.

Interviews complete the data collection. They have been
compared to the findings of the protocol analysis. In any case,
in the student interviews, we focused on their perceptions in
regards to their design cognition process and their learning
process. The focus in the teacher interview was on his/her perceptions of the interaction during the tutorial and his/her
own design cognition process. The interviews basically confirmed our findings.

The revision sessions we recorded, scripted and analyzed
basically have the same structure of content. The students describe their project, talking about the process through which
they aim to reach the solution they propose, the teacher eval-
uates the solution and proposes an alternative. At times the
students then agree or reply.

As we will see in next sections (see section 2.3), the protocols that we obtained were also the basis through which all
the analysis we needed was developed, in particular:
- identification of the problem solving models used;
- identification of the cognitive models that teachers and
  students apply.

2.1.2 Attendance and Summarization

Two courses that included Design Laboratory (Architectural Design and Building Elements' Technology) were monitored continuously in the Building Engineering and Architecture degree course of this university. In both courses, the design laboratory consists in the proposal of a design problem
that students have to solve, working in groups, through periodic revision sessions with the teachers.

The courses were analysed side by side with the teachers
during the frontal lessons and the revision sessions and collecting the work materials produced by the students in relation to the various design phases.

These "work in progress" materials were then scheduled
in order to organize a synthesis of the design process. Identifying learning steps and the students' advancing phases
during the elaboration of the design problem solution was
thus possible.

2.2. Design Learning: the Reference Reasoning Model

The understanding of the design process by means of cognitive models represents, in our opinion, one of the most fertile foundations of design education. In this paragraph, we
will introduce the cognitive model of design learning, which
has been defined according to of the one of the most relevant
psychological theories of reasoning – Johnson Laird's mental
models – and extended to well consolidated theories design
studies, like case based design. The model has been confirmed
by a number of experiments carried out analyzing the conceptual flows of a number of design stages through well-defined protocols. The model provides arguments supporting
the existence of at least three types of mental representations:
percepts, images, logical structures. The model shows that this
distinction is plausible from a functional analysis point of
view. We will develop arguments on the nature of mental
models to provide an integrated explanation of the cognitive
processes observed in qualified human performance in order
to have instruments to see how design can be traced back to a
series of well-defined cognitive activities.

2.2.1. A Reference Model of Human Mind

Cognitive science embraces a functional conception of the
mind that totally ignores the brain in its quality of "machine"
carrying out mental functions, and concentrates on the functional and operative emergence of the brain. It uses, as reference paradigms, the information theory, where the machines
finalized to the execution of a determined task can be represented in terms of the functions they carry out in order to
achieve their scope. The whole of the functions – in a certain
sense – capture the machines' interface with the outside
world, and in effect, represent an abstraction of it. It represents a model, to the point that structurally different machines can be considered equivalent, for analysis purposes, in
the moment in which they execute the same function. The
aim of cognitive psychology is to determine, through observation, the brain's functional emergence which we call mind,
and to induce its possible internal structure, principally using
the information theory paradigm.

Hence, one of the fundamental prerequisites of cognitive
science is that cognition consists in the manipulation of internal representations. In 1943, Craik wrote that from the information processing point of view, cognitive activity is
schematically made up of three principal processes:
* Comprehension: the translation of any external process in
  an internal representation in terms of words, numbers or
  actions.
* Reasoning: the derivation of other representations beginning with those generated by comprehension through
  whatever type of inferential process.
* Action: the retranslation of these symbols into actions, or
  at least an identification of the correspondence between
  external symbols and events.

The psychological basis of cognition therefore consists in
having in one's own mind the operative model of the real
phenomenon. If one understands what a building is, how a

certain mathematical demonstration is executed, the manner in which a computer works, flow dynamics or the passion for soccer, then one must have a mental representation that serves as model of the entity considered. In mental representations, the real phenomenon is imitated to maintain its relational structure, which is representing the entities and the relations in order to be able to imitate the phenomenon that regulated the functioning of the real equivalent. We will call these representations mental models. Mental models are at the basis of all the various processes of the mind that execute human reasoning. They make the organism capable of experimenting various alternatives, of deciding which of these is the best, of using knowledge of past events when dealing with present and future ones, and in general, they make it capable to react in a much more complete, safer and more adequate manner to the circumstances that occur.

Reduced scale models of reality do not need, in order to be useful, to be totally accurate nor do they need to correspond exactly to that which they portray. Our model of a coffee maker can reduce itself to the sole idea of a metal object which, opportunely filled with water, coffee and heated, produces coffee. If you were coffee maker designers, your model would also contain notions of fluid dynamics and technology of materials. Every model is thus complete in respect to one scope – for no empirical phenomenon will mental models exhaustive and adequate for every scope ever exist but, there will always be models that are more or less efficient. Therefore, it must not be taken for granted that adding information to models beyond a certain level increases their utility as well. Large part of our daily activity is regulated by simulations of real phenomenon that are extremely qualitative, useful only as long as the relation structure is sufficiently accurate for the predetermined aims.

2.2.2 Levels of Representation

If mental models are representations of reality, they are built on the basis of our experience of the world and therefore necessarily reflect the structure of the human cognitive system. In order to understand the nature of mental models, we must therefore necessarily build a reference cognitive structure, basing ourselves as far as possible on the more consolidated results of cognitive science and science in general. For our present aims, we will limit ourselves to a number of simple observations which, nevertheless, identify the principal functional emergence of the mind which, opportunely structured, form the mental processes we commonly observed during designing.

The most superficial level of interaction with reality occurs through the perceptive sphere. The primary receptors operate a codification of the stimulus coming from the outside world so as to build compatible signals capable of being elaborated by the higher level neuron layers. Monroe called this first level of representation Percept Level. Based on the type of stimulus, the perceptive sphere will be populated by fragments of sonar, visual, tactile and olfactory stimulation – opportunely selected and pre elaborated on the basis of the attentive control.

Carefully observe the image contained in fig. 3. Now close your eyes and mentally rotate the image 90° counter clockwise. Without observing the page again draw what you "observed". Read the text containing in fig. 3 a couple of times. Now, without looking at the page again, mentally repeat the verses. You will also be able to "listen" to the phonemes internally. What you experimented are so-called mental images. Mental images are representations organized by precepts that, in some way, contain the atomic semantic components – that is – the elements that isolated, do not express parts of meaning but isolate the portions of reality potentially relevant for the construction of the same. Images for every type of sense potentially exist. Visual images are therefore relative to entities and objects of the world. Sound images represent words, phrases, and speeches. Olfactory and tactile images, even if less common, can be equally structured. The structure of the visual mental images is less certain, as great variability in the detail level among the different subjects exists. In any case, the site of visual images represents a virtual space where it is possible, as we have done, to verify the relations and operate geometric transformations, and finally simulate spatial reality. In this way, we introduce a second representation level in our cognitive model called Image Level.

A human faculty related to images of particular interest, and perhaps limited to visual and hearing related images, is that of imagination: to imagine meanings to autonomously re-create mental images. Man is capable of autonomously recreating complex situations up to the point of constructing entire imaginary worlds. We commonly refer to these faculties as fantasy, because it is possible to construct situations without the bonds of perception that tie us inescapably to that which is real. If you close your eyes and think of a unicorn, you immediately understand what we are trying to say, because you will be able to answer questions such as: Does it look like horse? Is it white? Does it have wings? And so on. Therefore, to imagine is not to perceive, but the images are substantially by-products of the perceptive activity, in particular they are anticipatory phases of such activities, perceptive schemes that the receptors have distanced from the perceptive cycle for other scopes, and that represent invariants useful for the processes of reality comprehension. Imagination is not normally confused with perception because the latter implies the continuous harvesting of new information. Although the images reproduce structures coherent with reality, they do not contain meaning, intended in their more general level of "sense".

The construction of sense belongs to the third representation level, the Logical-Conceptual level. This is the level of the more abstract representations, where the categorical and operational structures of rational reasoning are contained. The faculty of language, intentionality and high level tasks such as problem solving and explanation are guided by the cognitive structures of the logical – conceptual level. The level its self is organized in mid levels; the number of which is potentially infinite. Think, for example, all of mathematical logics and of possible orders.

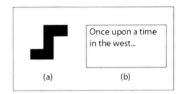

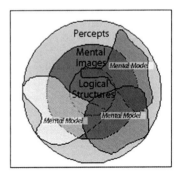

3.
Shape and a piece of text be used as mental images.

4.
Mental models and representations.

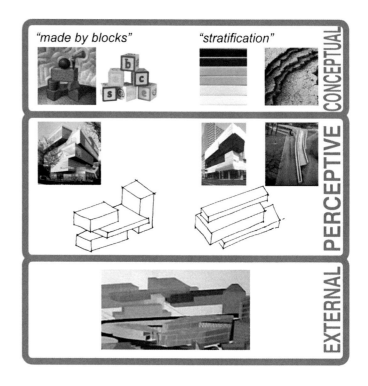

What is this mental model then? From our point of view, we can say that a mental model is a group of correlated representations, generally produced on three levels of cognitive sphere, directed at signifying a succession of symbols, or, in alternative, a state of the mind itself. The model is generated through the construction of representations correlated at different levels of abstraction. The correlation consists in the fact that each representation structures and/or specializes the representations of the lower level representation. This hierarchical organization of the representations is that which allows the model to simulate and hence foretell and/or imagine possible states of reality. This is where the models distinguish themselves from schemes. A scheme belongs to a single representation level, and carries out an important anticipation and construction function of local representation. There are, for example, perceptive schemes that guide attention in the selection of precepts and schemes-images that organize precepts in potentially significant wholes on the semantic level. A model is thus orthogonal to the three levels of the cognitive sphere. It organizes representations on different levels, in part regulated by schemes, and allows their reciprocal control. The mental models are thus at the basis of all the cognitive processes and have the extremely important capacity of correlating the various representation levels. This makes the complexity of human reasoning possible. In the mental rotation of the shape in fig. 3, for instance, in order to regulate the process at the image level we certainly used a logical scheme, given that the command called for a 90-degree counter clockwise rotation. Therefore, a translation of the concept of "nine-

5.
Signs and objects of building design domain arranged according to a multimodal perceptual representation.

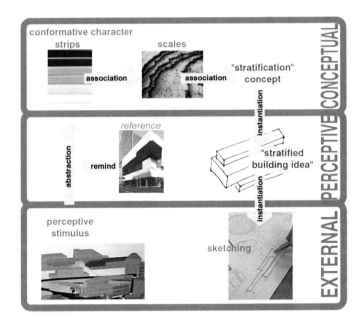

ty degrees" and "counter clockwise" certainly occurred in a whole of procedures and imagination faculty control activities. This coordination on different abstraction levels is what makes simulation and, more generally, reasoning by means of models possible.

2.2.3 Multimodal Perceptual Reasoning applied to Design

A number of studies deepened the application of mental model theory to design analysis. Chandrasekaran [Chandrasekaran 1999] called "Multimodal perceptual representation and diagrammatic reasoning" a cognitive model that views a "cognitive state" as an integrated and interlinked collection of "images" in various modalities: the perceptual ones, the kinaesthetic and conceptual modalities. Thinking, problem solving, reasoning, etc. are viewed as sequences of such states, where there is no intrinsically preferred mode.

So perception and imagination are deeply related processes that make use of internal representations called mental images. Mental images can be aggregated to form more complex patterns and/or abstracted to produce their logical interpretation. Mental images can also be reflected on external media (e.g. sketches on paper) and reinterpreted. Mental models are representation frames that aggregate sets of logical structures and the related mental images and characterize significant portions of the reality. Figure 5 shows a rearrangement of the mental images typical of a design process segment, according to a multimodal perceptual representation.

Also the teacher's interpretation of a student's drawing can, for example, be conceived according to a multimodal perceptual model as the construction of a mental model (fig. 6). This process starts from the abstraction of the external stimuli to form mental images. This usually results in a number of

6.
A functional schema of a multimodal perceptual model.

competing images. The emergence of one image over the others is related to the possibility of recalling analogous mental images from long term memory. The recalled image brings the entire set of associated mental models into the working memory. If the relations in the working memory are arranged coherently, the mental model is perceived as a representation of the external stimulus. In semiotic terms, the mental model, made of signs and of connoted objects, is the interpretative frame of the perceived object. So, to a certain extent, a cognitive model can be understood as a procedural model of the semiotic frame.

The interesting factor, in terms of design, is that even the opposite trail follows the same rules. The proposal that is, through a sketch of a new solution in this case, passes through the instantiation of a concept at the perceptive mental level (once again through the remind to other mental objects) and hence to its representation at the external stimuli level via a sketch.

2.2.4 Memory as a Storehouse

This leads us to consider the cognitive activity undertaken during mental imagery processing, in design persepctive. Visual mental imagery is seen as a perception of remembered information, not new input. More explicitly, images can be formed by activating visual memories of global patterns, by activating visual memories of individual parts and arranging them, or by selectively allocating attention [Kosslyn, 1995].

In our memory, mental images can be aggregated to form more complex models or can be abstracted to produce their logic interpretation. Thus, memory can be considered as a sort of dynamic archive that, as for a computer, accumulates and proposes each kind of content, also via images [Schank, 1982].

According to Tulvering's model [Konar, 2000], human memory is divided in three parts: sensorial memory that receive information, semantic memory for conceptual deductions, procedural memory that manages actions and processes coming out form sensorial and semantic memory. In the building design ambit, sensorial memory records information related to building perception, like viewing, hearing. Semantic memory contains ideas, aspects and features of design solutions and their connections, while procedural memory maintains interactions related to solving process and specifically connected with techniques used in the design process [Mubarak 2004].

The process that lets memory identify its proposal each time is analogical reasoning [Casakin & Goldschmidt 1999; Qian and Gero 1992; Chiu et al. 1997], that consists in the application of something that is contained in the memory to the objective that the designer is following. This association doesn't happen among superficial attributes but using "deep" features of the problem, each time constituting a sort of network between abstractions and analogies [Gentner 1983]. In other words, in order for our memory to return what it has stored at the right time, it is necessary that everything it archived was classified by its relevance in the related mental models, and that it was indexed.

2.3 Design Learning Practice Analysis: Achievements

Design Learning Practice Analysis through these two perspectives enabled us to identify some considerations regarding Design Learning Models generally occurring in Traditional Design Education.

First of all we have to consider that, as a number of research found, all these design process aspects are more developed and elaborated in experts' work, while novices are still weak in one or another of these steps or stages. For this reason, very often and especially during design revision sessions, the teacher (expert) suggests or addresses the student (novice) to resolving concept or reference cases. But in this way it is not certain that the student understands the teacher's instructions. In fact, novices often have not yet acquired the interpretative code of the specific domain which, on the other hand, is used automatically by the experts. Furthermore, as Legrenzi underlines, "...the experts themselves often are not able to explain the cognitive bonds of their abilities (...), who designs and realizes artefacts that face human needs today cannot ignore cognitive psychology" [Legrenzi in Arielli, 2003]

In our research, we have considered how students and teacher deal with the Design Cognitive Process, pointing out the different perspectives of expert and novice. As far as the design cognition process is concerned, the cognitive process of expert and novice follows different paths: the expert manages to consider the problem as a whole and considers the problem in terms of interaction with the sub-problems, whereas novices are not able to see the whole problem, they tend to decompose it and find specific solutions to sub-problems which are sometimes inconsistent. Moreover, the use of precedents differs, since the novice sees them in terms of the image of the final product, while the expert considers them in terms of the process that has produced that image. Anyhow, the necessity and usefulness of the provision of a case library, possibly classified on the basis of process rather than product, seems important.

Secondly, as to the tutorial discourse and pedagogical model, although there is particular attention on encouraging and motivating feedback, the tutorial dialogue lacks the eliciting/soliciting move that forms part of the scaffolding phase and could be crucial in the promotion of self-learning on the students' part. It does not encourage students to actively construct their knowledge, nor leaves space to the genuine interaction that could create knowledge.

Design Cognition Process
Through protocol analysis our observations have confirmed that the main part of the work, especially in the initial phases of design activities, consists in the construction of the design problem space. Below we can see the main issues that emerged through the protocol analysis.

Macro Strategies
Both the students and the teacher follow the same co-evolution model for design problem solving:

- Problem Scoping/representation
- Developing alternative solutions
- Realization

however, their operative strategies differ seeing that the teacher applies a typical *multimodal perceptual design reasoning* (see paragraph 2.2.3) (fig. 7) where he/she starts from a conceptual representation of all the problem elements and constraints and returns once and again to the perceptual level through sketches of partial solutions, trying to find a concrete solution that could turn his/her concepts and mental images into a synthetic solution assisted by references to precedents.

The students, on the other hand, failed to see a synthetic solution from the elements and constraints of the problem posing and did not reach the conceptual level just "sitting" on the perceptual level (fig. 8).

Students set a criteria or an image, which is generally arbitrarily chosen, and applied it to the context, without going back to the conceptual level but using a precedent as a model to imitate and apply to their contextual situation. In other words, they did not show and/or use any of the critical representational frames of the precedent design solution they had chosen. As a matter of fact, the choice of the precedent was not made on the basis of the process that produced such a product, rather on the basis of the image of the product, which could roughly suit their context. The teacher made reference to precedents at the end of the session generally; it does not appear that he/she had a predefined idea of which case might have been used to solve that particular problem. The teacher's experience made creating a mental image of the solution possible, an image which automatically or unconsciously referred back to that particular precedent.

Furthermore, referring always to Multimodal Perceptual Reasoning, protocol analysis has shown that associative thought appears to be the main reasoning type. Association links concepts and images, but once the association is established new insights and unexpected solutions may be stimulated. This implies that images are only vague representations of the visual stimuli and only the presence of fully developed external stimuli trigger the development of

7.
Teacher's design process: multimodal perceptual design reasoning.

8.
Student's design process.

E-LEARNING FOR ARCHITECTURE

new abstract representations. Schematic representations play an important role in the design process, as well. They arrange images into classes and bridge the image level and the conceptual level through a codification of percept that abstract from unnecessary details and focus on few, and semantically well defined, features. The emergence of one image over another is related to the possibility of reminding analogous mental images from the long term memory. Sketching also plays an important role, triggering the mental imagery creation and processing.

Micro Strategies

When the teacher proposed or suggested an alternative solution he/she generally followed these steps:

Developing tentative solution that becomes more definite through sketches and gestures. Verbalization at this stage is scarce. At times, it develops through the interaction with the students, but most often it evolves by means of rhetorical questions, individual reflection and individual thought and evaluations.

Clarifying the solution through sketches, movements, actions on the model, giving details and explanations

Justifying the solution using application knowledge and going back to the conceptual level.

The students never suggested solutions, but generally repeated or confirmed the comprehension of the teacher's suggestions thus establishing that the level of knowledge is shared and the conversation could proceed, as well as completing or anticipating the teacher's utterance.

Reflection in action

The revision sessions are a way for the students to reflect on what they produced, and on the process that made it possible. It is a conscious and rational action that can lead to reframing the problem, making new moves or attending new issues. This process takes place in the revision sessions but it is carried out by the teacher, who interacts with the material and has to verbalize his/her process in order to make it clear to the students. The design problem is actually reframed and new moves are made to solve it, which not always spring from the students proposed solution.

Gestures and sketches

Gestures and sketches are mainly iconic and tend to emphasize or reinforce the meanings that need to be conveyed. The teacher's drawings especially are very schematic, lines of circles, rough and imprecise, which seemed to be only supporting his/her thinking activity. Interestingly, although the drawings seemed rather pointless, from a first look at the interviews the students claimed that the most helpful aid from the teacher were his sketches and drawings.

In the whole, we have to highlight that in several protocol analysis experiments conducted so far, the segments relative to the phase in which the teacher tried to propose alternative design solutions are always very interesting. In this phase the teacher, in substance, set off a design micro process starting

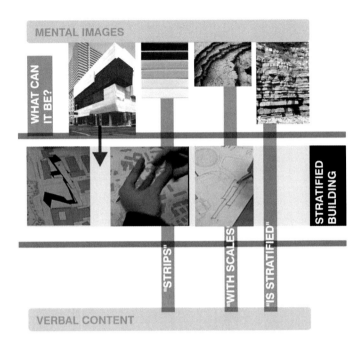

MENTAL IMAGES

WHAT CAN IT BE?

STRATIFIED BUILDING

"STRIPS" "WITH SCALES" "IS STRATIFIED"

VERBAL CONTENT

from the student's drawings, generally selecting and addressing only certain issues.

For instance, in the design fragment described through the figures, the teacher should have provided the students with hints regarding the aggregative character of volumes. In this case, it was observed that the teacher was not able to clarify the issue until he developed an alternative solution to the student design problem. In this segment, the ongoing definition of the resolving concept regarding the "stratified building" is clearly observable (fig. 9). The gradual character of the event is signalled via the teacher's altering in his/her attempt to visualize the problem and his/her definition through gestures, words, recalling of references and mental images and through the elaboration of sketches.

Only via this "reflection in action" phase can he/she rationalize the concept (e.g. "stratified building") from the cognitive point of view which he/she will then be capable of suggesting to the student.

On the other side, protocol analysis from the students' side demonstrates that it is neither immediate nor certain that the student grasps what the teacher wants to communicate precisely. The observation of subsequent revision protocols demonstrated how communication between teacher and student is not always efficient. In our case for instance, the concept of "stratification" did not have the same significance for the teacher as it did for the student, and only after a number of revisions did the student grasp the sense of what the teacher was saying.

9.
Functional scheme that synthesizes the interaction between various forms of expressions in a solutions' elaboration process.

The recurring problem in the revisions observed is basically related to teacher/student communication and it presents two components. The first component is semantic and consists in the fact that an interpretive code which allows efficient communication is not usually shared between the two subjects.

In fact, semantic analysis highlighted many incoherencies between graphic, verbal mnemonic representation of the same concept and, in general, it identified an extremely low associative capacity in the student. The principal cause for this problem is the lack of a clear knowledge structure in the student which allows him to decode the problem and the lack of a "reference storehouse" to which he/she can efficiently turn to in order to allow him/her to elaborate successful solutions.

A second, more cognitive component, consists in the fact that while the teacher, thanks to his/her experience, passes automatically to the conceptual level and has the significance relationships clear, the student often stops at the perceptual level – failing to understand the sense of what the teacher proposes in the revision.

Once again this problem can be initially traced back to the students' lack of an adequate knowledge framework which would allow him/her to decode the problem in a structured manner. It can also be traced back to the students' lack of experience determining the fact that he/she does not usually activate via abstraction, association and instantiation processes.

Always considering our example, we do a comparison between the process which the student put into practice ("observed process") and the ideal process which he/she should have put into practice ("suggested process"). The ideal process can occur only through the scaffolding of the students' activity and of the trail he/she pursued.

Tutorial Discourse

Turns
The interaction takes place within the following average time frame (Table 1):

Table 1: Interaction time frame

0: 00	6: 00	11: 00	12: 00	14: 00	17: 00
Students	**Teacher**	**Interaction**	**Teacher**		**Interaction**
Problem definition and introduction of a preliminary solution	Evaluation and tentative solution proposed	Problem space reframed	Clarification and justification		Confirm comprehension and suggestion of precedents

Acts
From the chart it is clear how unbalanced the time distribution between teacher and students is. This suggests that "non interactive" acts occur quite frequently. Of course, the most critical interactions for the meaningful construction of

knowledge, like scaffolding, are not exploited. As far as the evaluation move is concerned, the teacher performed it as follows:

- highlighting correct aspects,
- pointing out the incorrect ones
- explaining the reason
- giving possible solution.

Discourse Strategies

While the problem space is reframed through a short interaction with the students, the students did not actually intervene much. They only kept the channel of communication open, using discourse strategies to confirm comprehension like rephrasing, repeating or using ok. The teacher instead lectured most of the time: thought aloud, expressed his opinion, commented, suggested, gave directions, asked rhetorical questions, asked for confirmation. He/she rarely elicited or solicited responses from the students or uses other scaffolding instrument to make them improve or elaborate their solution.

3. DESIGN E-LEARNING COURSES REQUIREMENTS

3.1 Critical points for design e-learning corse

In this context, thinking about e-learning appear more difficult than with other subjects, because of the amount of competence, in termo f knowledge and skill, that are usually transmitted via the studio work approach, the day-by-day closeness between expert and novice.

In particolar, it is possible to highlight three main critical points to consider in the perspective of e-learning corse requirement definition:

Critical learning. A/E/C education is mainly focuses on the Design Process, with a strong professional character of the learning project, with a poor attention to cognitive aspects of education. In traditional learning the transmission of this specific critical level and of the related comptences is mainly put down to the revision session practice, using the "learning by doing" cognitive model. However, not always teachers can evaluate specifically how much the students actually learn, that is what they bring in their cognitive fund so that they could apply it autonomously. In the case of on-line courses this aspect is even more delicate, because the transmission of competences that in traditional learning occurs side by side in the homework revision session has to be "translated" in the e-learning lesson, that is give a problematic perspective to the critical information that usually are transmitted by the teacher (abstraction and correlation to the critical level of the problem) and that have to be put in the lesson's structure. In this perspective the relation among learning models and knowledge framework has a central role.

Semantic Relevance of Contents. Main problem joined to the use of on-line learning materials are for learners are cognitive overload, disorientation and distraction, poor narrative flow, and poor conceptual flow. To overcome these problems, e-learners need support in retrieving and evaluating online information, that could introduce a second level of knowledge representation, a semantic layer, that aim to index the semantic content of the knowledge contained in a lesson course. In this way each architectural object will be represented by a set of interpretative models that point out relevant aspects in the different view point.

Association and Correlation. On-line courses risk to become "flat" because of the lack of semantic layer and conceptual correlation, that a computer cannot define. It is strictly necessary that courses were managed via associative-conceptual relations among their contents and architectural object. In this way they will be able to provide to learners the key concept for the critical interpretation of information and to teachers a management and maintenance tool for information and knowledge.

3.2 Scaffolding Guidelines for Design Learning

The analisys carried on in precedent sections shows that design e-learning courses has to offer not only informations and knowledge but also perspective on them, semantic relevance and correlation; not only **the** *content* of traditional courses but also the *critical contribution* that in traditional learning is offered "automatically" and "indirecty" by the teachers.

So, the main interest of e-learning on design is not the "transposition" of the same contents by means of new technological instruments but the identification of guidelines for the structure of e-learning courses, in order to make them fully comprehensible and exploitable in terms of competence, knowledge and skills.

In the learning research context this kind of operation is called scaffolding.

The term "scaffolding" was introduced in psychology studies by Jerome Bruner in 1976, and it indicates all that supporting and leading strategies for the learning processes that enable to carry out a task also without the complete set of required competences, because of the aid of an expert that provides suggestions and indications, waiting for a complete autonomy in the task development.

Scaffolding is a mechanism that assists learners in extending their learning into more complex or unknown

areas of knowledge and knowledge application (such as real-life problems). Scaffolds may take many

forms including learner guides, resources, tools and strategies that help the learner attain higher levels

of understanding. Scaffolding often takes the form of modelling, coaching and questioning to

lead students through the problem solving task [Hmelo-Silver, 2004]. In order to define the instruments and procedures that are useful as "scaffolding" for the learning of design, two different types of operations are needed:
- accompanying/guiding the student step-by-step in *explicating the reasoning processes* in order to lead him/her up to the conceptual level.

- help him/her build the vastest interpretive code possible, that is, help him/her acquire a *vast and flexible knowledge structure* which he/she knows also how to visualize via reference cases.

3.2.1 Reasoning Process Scaffolding

Accordingly, our study may suggest a number of guidelines in order to make novices' cognitive processes closer to experts', thus improving the teaching and learning process both in presence and in distant-online learning. As we have pointed out, the tutoring frame is mirrored only in its structure during revision session. The critical aspect is the lack of students' active involvement and their interaction with teachers. This happens when teachers, after the identification of a student's design error, naturally develops the correct solution thinking aloud. In this way teachers convey a rich pre-assembled design solution strategy, made of the sketching (i.e. perceptual level) and critical apparatus (i.e. conceptual level). However, not coming from the student's original elaboration, the solution is not learned (i.e. interiorized). Consequently the student is not able to reuse the learned solution in a critical way (e.g. in different design contexts) and the observed students' behaviour is a sort of blind imitation of the teachers' behaviour.

As far as concerns leading the student step-by-step we propose the following stages for carrying out scaffolding:
- Abstraction: The teacher gives feedback to the student's design project interpreting student's design through a set of relevant abstract schemata.
- Internalizing: the teacher asks the students to map the abstract schemata, requesting them to explicit the correspondences among elements of the schema and their design instantiation. In this way the students interiorize the teacher's conceptual apparatus.
- Evaluation: the teacher points out strengths and weakness of the students' design by criticizing the interpretation schemata. Errors and good solutions are identified at the abstract level.
- Solution: The teacher asks the students to synthesize a solution schema either by completely reformulating some of the interpretative schemata or partially correcting them. This is a complex phase and often requires a recursive activation of the entire design process. Students often get stuck in this phase. In this case, it is necessary to help the students by proposing a set of possible solution schemata and asking them to select the one they believe to be the best.
- Instantiation: The teacher asks the students to instantiate the abstract solution schemata into detailed design representations (i.e. drawings, paintings, etc.).

Thus, it seems evident that, for e-learning it is necessary to predispose systems and tools that could provide to learners these *abstract solution schemata* as reference, in order to lead them also in the conceptual level, interiorizing not only the contents but also their operational relevance.

3.2.2 Design Knowledge Structure acquiring

In some sense didactic is the art of mediating knowledge structures into learning processes. Authentic learning contextualises knowledge creation and application, and with strong scaffolding and support, can be highly motivational to learners and encourage participation [Herrington et al., 2003].

Therefore, in order to design a didactic strategy one need to understand what is the structure and the nature of the knowledge involved in the subject one is going to teach. So it's really important to devote special attention to the representation of design knowledge. In design, the knowledge types are highly diverse and domain sensitive. We can classify design knowledge according to three dimension:
- the aspect of the domain it describes,
- the role it plays in the design processes,
- the supporting media.

A fundamental distinction occurs through the first dimension among declarative/conceptual knowledge (knowing what is), procedural knowledge (knowing how to) and strategic knowledge (meta-cognitive).
- Declarative/Conceptual Knowledge: It consists essentially of facts, objects, situations describing components, structures and functions, theorems, etc. Declarative knowledge can be abstract, when it describes a concept or a generally relevant fact, or situated, when it describes a unique occurrence of a fact (e.g. a design case), or a relevant instantiation of a general concept (e.g. an application of a compositive theme to a particular situation).
- Procedural Knowledge: It consists of operating rules, procedures, methods, describing how to proceed in the accomplishment of a given task. Procedural knowledge can be abstract or situated. Abstract procedural knowledge usually captures best-practices, which describe how to solve general and relevant tasks. Situated procedural knowledge describes the accomplishment of a given task in a well defined context.
- Strategic Knowledge: Strategic (meta-cognitive) knowledge represent a second order, how to, that is how to reason in order to design or to solve a problem. It is aimed at representing expertise. When strategic knowledge is provided the learning process receives a speed up and learning occurs more effectively. The role of strategic knowledge is therefore fundamental. We consider strategic (meta-cognitive) knowledge as the basic means for expertise transfer.

According to the second dimension we have a plethora of possible knowledge roles, depending on the associated processes. Some examples are:
- General Design: Requirement, Regulation, Goal, Solution, Failure, etc.;
- Case Based Design: Issues, Concepts, Precedents or Cases, etc.;
- Process Management: Status, Action, Constraint, etc.;
- General Purpose Inference: Concept, Relation, etc.

Paragraphs

Semantic Level

Searching and Coaching Procedures

According to the third dimension we can have the usual formats of surface representation: Texts, Hyper-Texts, Images, Drawings, and Videos.

As far as concerns the acquisition of a vast, flexible and visible knowledge structure, it is fundamental that instruments providing students with vast repertories of reference cases be set up. In particular, these need to be indexed according to well structured class structures and critically articulated so that the examples can be easily traced and associated – at the conceptual level – with the problematic issues which the student must address. In fact, not always an information received can be stored as knowledge, especially if this information has not got any association through the various knowledge levels. In order to ensure knowledge acquiring a scaffolding system has to propose and manage a great amount of association between materials, contents and information.

3.3 A proposal for design e-learning courses

The effectiveness and efficiency of web based learning for both learners and instructors depend crucially on the organization of the on-line learning resources, which determines the easiness of their creation and retrieval. Currently available online educational materials, such as electronic text books and web-based courses, are mostly hypertexts containing hierarchical links that represent the book or course structure, and possibly, simple transversal links from pages to associated (similar) pages [Dichev et al., 2004]. The main problem related to using educational hypertexts for learners are cognitive overload, disorientation and distraction, poor narrative flow, and poor conceptual flow [Jacobson et al., 1996]. To overcome these problems, e-learners need support in retrieving and evaluating online information. This requires a new organization of web resources.

Our proposal introduces a second layer of knowledge representation, the semantic layer aimed at indexing the semantic content of the knowledge contained in a course. The semantic layer is just behind the surface layer that contains that which will be presented to the learners (fig. 10).

Two pilot lessons have been detailed as mock-up for the technological development of the hypothesized e-learning methodology. They have been implemented via power point slides, simulating the basic functionality of a on-line system. The objective of the pilot lessons is to show the usefulness and efficiency of the knowledge-structure-based indexing in the development of on-line lessons with a rich interconnection.

From a methodological point of view, the idea was associating to all the contents in the database (for the lessons) a sort of descriptive label. The label is composed of two parts: a index for the actual knowledge class, that is a word that identify the information type (e.g. "functional typology" or "materials") and a value, that is the actual descriptive information (e.g. "museum" or "copper and glass"). The labels rule the associative relations among all the contents and enable a navigation among conceptual correlations.

10.
Semantic level.

BIBLIOGRAPHY

Arielli E. (2003). *Pensiero e progettazione. La psicologia cognitiva applicata al design e all'architettura*. Mondadori, Milano.

S. Bhatta and A. Goel, From Design Experiences to Generic Mechanisms: Model-Based Learning in Analogical Design,. In Proceedings of the AID-94 workshop on Machine Learning in Design, Aug. 1994, Lausanne, Switzerland.

Blessing, L. T. M. (1994). A process-based approach to computer-supported engineering design. Universiteit Twente, Enschede.

Casakin, H., Goldschmidt, G. (1999). Expertise and the use of visual analogy: implications for design education. *Design Studies,* Vol. 20, No. 2, pp. 153-175.

Chiu, M-L. and Shih, S-G. (1997). Analogical Reasoning and Case Adaptation in Architectural Design: Computers vs. Human Designers. In: *CAAD Futures 1997*, Proceedings of the 7th International Conference on Computer Aided Architectural Design Futures, Munich, Germany, pp.787-800.

Chandrasekaran B. (1990). Design Problem Solving: a Task Analysis. *AI Magazine*, 11 (4): 59-71.

Chandrasekaran, B., Johnson, T. R. (1993). Generic tasks and task structures: History, critique and new directions. In J.-M. David, J.-P. Krivine, & R. Simmons (Ed.), *Second Generation Expert Systems*. Springer-Verlag, Berlin.

Chandrasekaran, B. (1999). Multimodal perceptual representation and design problem solving. In: *Proc. Of Visual and spatial reasoning in design: computational and cognitive approaches*, 15-17 June 1999, MIT, Cambridge, USA.

Cross N. (2004), Expertise in design an overview, Design Studies Volume 25, Issue 5, September 2004, Pages 427-441

Darses, F. (1990c). Constraints in design: towards a methodology of psychological analysis based on AI Formalisms. Paper presented at the INTERACT'90, North Holland

De Bra P., Calvi L. (1998). AHA! An open adaptive hypermedia architecture, *The New review of Multimedia and Hypermedia*, (4), p.115-139

De Grassi, M., Giretti, A., Pinese, P. (1999). Knowledge Structures of Episodic Memory in Architectural Design: an Example of Protocol Analysis. *Proceedings of the 17th eCAADe conference*, September 1999, Liverpool.

De Grassi, M., Giretti, A., Mengoni, M. (2005). Modelling Design E-learning environments through observation of designers. Gero J. Eds, In: *Proceedings of International Workshop on Observing Designers*, Aix En Provence, France.

Dichev C., Dicheva D., & Aroyo L. (2004). Using Topic Maps for Web-based Education, Int. J. Advanced Technology for Learning, Vol. 1, No 1, 2004, 1-7.

Ericsson, K. A., & Simon, H. A. (1993). *Protocol analysis; Verbal reports as data*. Bradford books/MIT Press, Cambridge, MA.

Gentner, D., (1983), Structure mapping: a Theoretical Framework for Analogy. *Cognitive Science*, Vol 7, No 2, pp. 155-170.

Gero, J. S. (1990). Design prototypes: a knowledge representation schema for design. AI Magazine, 11 (4), 26-36.

Gero, J. (Ed.). (1991). Artificial Intelligence in Design '91. Oxford: Butterworth-Heinemann.

Gero, J. S. (Ed.). (1992). Artificial Intelligence in Design '92. Boston: Kluwer.1998

P. Lloyd and P. Scott, Discovering the Design Problem. Design Studies 15 (1994), pp. 125–140.

Gero, J. S. (1998). Conceptual designing as a sequence of situated acts. In I. Smith (Ed.), Artificial Intelligence in structured engineering (pp. 165-177). Berlin

Gero, J. (1998). Towards a model of designing which includes its situatedness. In H. Grabowski, S. Rude & G. Grein (Eds.), Universal design theory (pp. 47-56). Aachen (Germany): Shaker Verlag.

Gero, J. S. (1998). Conceptual designing as a sequence of situated acts. In I. Smith (Ed.), Artificial

Intelligence in structured engineering (pp. 165-177). Berlin: Springer.

Hmelo-Silver, C. E. (2004). Problem-based learning: What and how do students learn. *Educational Psychology Review*, Vol. 16 No. 3, pp. 235-266

Jacobson M., Maouri C., Mishra P., Kolar C. (1996). Learning with hypertext learning environment, *Journal of Educational Multimedia and Hypermedia*, (5), p.239-281

Kavakli, M., Gero, J.S. (2001). Sketching as mental imagery processing. *Design Studies*, Vol. 22 (4): 347-364.

Konar, A. (2000). *Artificial Intelligence and Soft Computing: Behavioral and Cognitive Modeling of the Human Brain*, CRC Press, Florida.

Kosslyn, S.M. (1995). Mental Imagery. In Kosslyn, S.M. and D.N. Osherson (eds) *An Invitation to Cognitive Science, Visual Cognition*, 2nd edition MIT Press, Cambridge MA

Kosslyn, S.M. and D.N. Osherson (eds) (1995). An *Invitation to Cognitive Science, Visual Cognition*, 2nd edition MIT Press, Cambridge MA

Logan, B., & Smithers, T. (1993). Creativity and design as exploration. In Gero & M. L. Maher (Eds.), Modeling creativity nad knowledge-based design (pp. 193-175). Hillsdale, NJ: Erlbaum93

Maher, M.L., and Balachandran, B. Zhang D.M. (1995), Case Based Reasoning in Design, Lawrence Earlbaum, New Jersey

Mubarak, K. (2004). *Case Based Reasoning for Design Composition in Architecture*, PhD dissertation, Carnegie Mellon University School of Architecture.

Newell, A. (1966). *On the analysis of human problem solving protocols.* Carnegie Mellon University, Department of Computer Science, Pittsburgh, Pa.

Novak, J. D. (1977). *A Theory of Education.* Cornell University Press, Ithaca, NY.

Novak, J. D., D. B. Gowin. (1984). *Learning How to Learn.* Cambridge University Press, Cambridge, UK.

Novak, J. D., & J. Wandersee, 1991. Coeditors, Special Issue on Concept Mapping of Journal of Research in Science Teaching, 28, 10

Oxman Rivka E. (1994) "Precedents in Design: a Computational Model for the Organization of Precedent Knowledge", Design Studies, Vol.15, No.2, pp. 141-157

Pahl, G., & Beitz, W. (1996). Engineering design. A systematic approach (K. M. Wallace, Blessing & F. Bauert, Trans. 2nd, enlarged and updated ed.). London: Springer

Quin L., and Gero, J. (1992). A Design Support System Using Analogy, In: *Proc. Second Int'l Conf. AI in Design*, Kluwer Academic Publishers, Dordrecht, The Netherlands, pp. 795 –813.

Schank, C.R. (1982). *Dynamic memory. A theory of reminding and learning in computers and people.* Cambridge University Press, MA.

Schank C.R. (1992) Goal-Based Scenarios, Technical Report No.36, Institute for Learning Sciences, Northwestern University.

Schank C.R. (1992) Goal-Based Scenarios, Technical Report No.36, Institute for Learning Sciences, Northwestern University.

Schön, D. A. (1983). The reflective practitioner: How professionals think in action. New York: Basic Books (reprinted in 1995).

Schön, D. A. (1984). The design studio: An exploration of its traditions and potentials. London: RIBA

Schön, D. A. (1992, March). Designing as reflective conversation with the materials of a design situation. Knowledge-Based Systems, 5 (1), 3-14. 92

Schreiber, A. Th., Wielinga, B. J., Akkermans, H., Van Der Velde, W., & Hoog, R. de (1994). CommonKADS, A comprehensive methodology for KBS development, Deliverable ESPRIT project P5248, KADS-II/DM1.2a. (Ext. r. no.). Amsterdam: Universiteit van Amsterdam

Simon, H. A. (1973/1984). The structure of ill-structured problems. Artificial Intelligence, 1973, 4, 181-201.

The sciences of the artificial (3rd, rev. ed. 1996; Orig. ed. 1969; 2nd, rev. ed. 1981) (3 ed.). Cambridge, MA: The MIT Press.

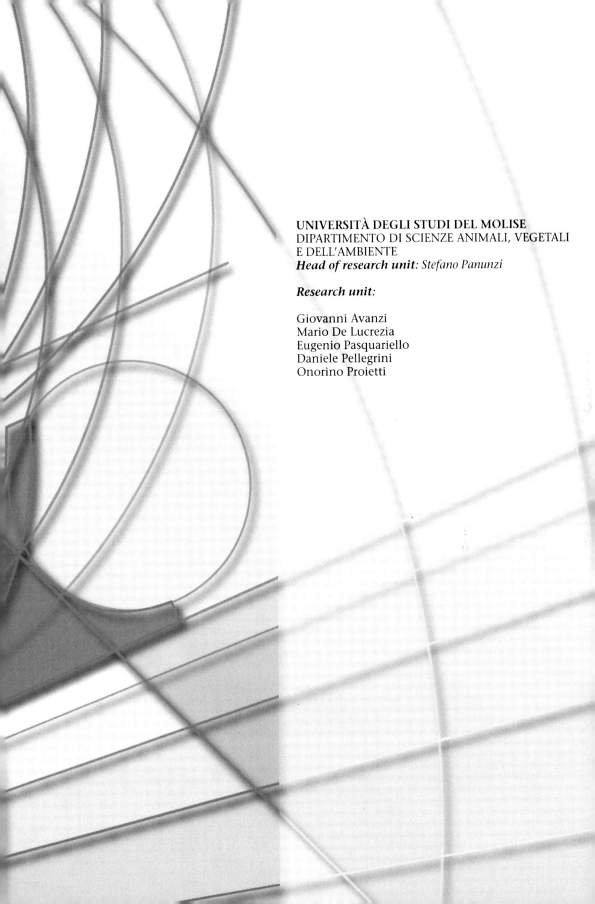

UNIVERSITÀ DEGLI STUDI DEL MOLISE
DIPARTIMENTO DI SCIENZE ANIMALI, VEGETALI
E DELL'AMBIENTE
Head of research unit: Stefano Panunzi

Research unit:

Giovanni Avanzi
Mario De Lucrezia
Eugenio Pasquariello
Daniele Pellegrini
Onorino Proietti

The design of telecontiguity systems for distance learning

STEFANO PANUNZI

INTRODUCTION

> *"Je ne sais si jamais philosophe a revé d'une société pour*
> *la distribution de Réalité Sensible à domicile"*
> La conquete de l'ubiquité, Paul Valéry, 1928

> *"The television screen received and transmitted*
> *at the same time"*
> 1984, George Orwell, 1949

> *"The appearance of the surfaces disguises*
> *a secret transparency, a thickness without depth"*
> Improbable Architecture, Paul Virilio, 1983

Walter Benjamin maintained that, like the cinema, "architecture supplies material for a simultaneous collective reception". The unexpected confusion between the reception of images emitted by a cinema projector and the perception of architectural forms is a clear indication of the significance of the current transformation of the idea of 'surface', of 'face to face', which, as we have noted, leads to the disappearance of the interface. The 'new office' is no longer a room, but only a screen, a viewing-desk. The interruption and subdivision of physical space is rapidly replaced by the interruption of emission and reception. Space is thus produced and projected by visual shots that are also shots in time, in the tele-topological continuum of projection and reception at a distance. The appearance of the surfaces by now disguises a secret transparency, a thickness without depth.

Espace Critique – Improbable architecture, Paul Virilio, 1983

The major source of interest of Internet lies in its capacity to transmit images on a global scale, to be able to use live-cams that show images in real time that have been taken practically everywhere. If the industrial revolution raised the issues of serialisation and standardisation, the information and communication revolution poses the question of synchronicity. Synchronicity means giving a form to time: to the time of interactivity and connectivity; it confronts architecture with questions which have never been asked before. Architecture thus has to be able to translate the 'face to face of all surfaces' into connectivity, inter– connections, interactiveness. The importance of real time compared to the surfaces of real space is fundamental, because time predominates over real space. Space will always be present, but will be de-qualified by the time of the speed of light, by connectivity, by inter-connections, interactiveness. Thus from now on city architecture has to be an architecture of time and of feedback, not only an architecture of space and surfaces. To-

1.a
Public demonstration of the prototype with internet link on the Campus of the Università degli Studi del Molise – XVI Scientific and Technological Culture Week MIUR – 2006.

1.b
Link-up between the Rome Aquarium (Rome Architects Association) and the Information Science Room of Termoli University campus (Università degli Studi del Molise) – 2008.

1.c
Link up between the Department of Architecture (Sapienza Università di Roma) and the Information Science Room of Termoli University campus (Università degli Studi del Molise) – 2008.

day we are about to pass into a real time perspective; the perspective of real space obviously continues to exist and to be important.
Towards an architecture of feedback, interview of Paul Virilio by François Burkhardt for issue n° 1 of the review *Crossing*, 2000

1.1 Telecontiguity: tangible videoconferencing

The term *telecontiguity*[1] relates to the experimental didactic research of Information Communication Technology (ICT) as applied to architecture and urban spaces, led by and coordinated by Stefano Panunzi, primary researcher and teacher in the Faculty of Architecture of the Sapienza University of Rome[2], and co-founder of the Faculty of Engineering of the Università degli Studi del Molise, where he has been able to create a functioning prototype *telecontiguity* system. This system, which is a natural evolution in videoconferencing, is unique in its kind and represents an Italian achievement that is totally competitive at an international level in its effectiveness, simplicity and economic cost, compared to similar research in the field of telepresence in Europe, the United States, Canada and Japan[3].

The research carried out by the Unit of the Università degli Studi del Molise within the scope of Research PRIN 2006 aimed at perfecting the *telecontiguity* system to create an interactive screen. *Telecontiguity* can be regarded as the new frontier of telepresence in that it can transform a simple pane of glass into a shared tangible surface for video-communication. The tangibility lies in the fact that a person can approach the screen and even touch it, while continuing to be visible where they actually are and retaining their actual dimensions, without the limits of positioning/distance/framing that are found in normal videoconferencing. The screen literally 'sees', or rather films, whatever is in front of it, like a scanner; in fact, the image of whatever is in contact with the glass is in perfect 1: 1 scale. The participants can thus communicate face to face at the normal distance of a natural conversation, and can look each other in the eye as if they were separated merely by a pane of glass; there is a reciprocal contact between both sides at the scale of 1: 1. This novel technological system guarantees that there is a mutual correspondence between the two transmitted and received images by setting up a 'fourth wall'in common to both spaces, making them appear contiguous and adjoining, even though in reality they are far apart. The possible applications are incalculable; in the specific field of teaching design, experiments have been carried out that allowed several people to talk to one another face to face, produce designs simultaneously and build models that were half on one side and half on the other. This system of *telecontiguity* is particularly effective when setting up an audio-visual juxtaposition surface which can coincide with such elements of architectonic and urban space as doors, windows, walls, facades, etc., and that can be regarded as a supplement to a real space (*augmented reality*: see Flavia Sparacino MIT, USA) without any need to darken the surroundings.

1.2 Teaching and the proxemics of design reviewing

In the teaching of architecture, one of the most important and intricate moments in teacher-student interaction is without a doubt the reviewing of the students' designs, where collaboration and a simultaneous involvement with the *learning objects* are paramount. One of the most perplexing problems, found in the majority of evaluations of distance learning in architecture, is in fact the lack of *face to face* interaction between student and teacher.

Videoconferencing has tried to rectify this deficiency, but has not solved the problem of *critical distance* in *face to face* communication (T. Hall), where the participants can have eye contact and where a *critical distance* is maintained between their two bodies[4]. To a certain extent the emotional tension that exists in a live dialogue between two people is missing in normal videoconferencing; the real/virtual space in which the communication takes place is cold and distant. It is no accident that video-telephony has not been a success story, even in its more recent version of video-chat.

The absence of interaction in live design reviewing has diminished the educational value of distance learning; at times it has been actually discontinued precisely because of its lack of emotional involvement. Videoconferencing has proved to be so far the only system that has been able to recreate certain aspects of telepresence, and this system has been the object of the *interaction design* dealt with by this Research Unit. Interfaces should be designed to be simple, with a high level of perceptibility, in order to comply with usability and ergonomic guidelines. One primary objective is the introduction of an effective interactive component into on-line learning and also the creation of learning forms and methods that are highly emotionally involving and which are developed within a collaborative environment. In recent years interaction design has become of great interest to designers of platforms and e-learning applications. A specific skill is thus being developed, to be applied in the design of teaching and learning environments; the system that the user interacts with is an essential part of the process. This system should be designed on the basis of usability and also according to principles regarding use experience. There is a need to create systems and interfaces that continuously engage the attention and require a constant interaction on the part of the user. The designing of an e-learning environment means following a non-linear path where one is continuously faced with the complexity of the learning situation; it is a recursive process, open to continual supplementation.

Design reviewing, especially in the case of the teaching of architecture, always has an initial stage of classroom teaching followed by a series of periodic individual meetings between

2.a-b-c
Testing of the superimposed desktop graphics between the Department of Architecture (Sapienza Università di Roma) and the Information Science Room of Termoli University campus (Università degli Studi del Molise) – 2008.

the teacher and student, for an in-progress discussion of their design plans. This extremely important stage cannot be restricted or modified in any way; it has to respect the timescales and traditional methods of a dialogue between teacher and student, where standardised procedures and results do not exist. The teacher has to be able to understand the student's intentions and to help him to translate his intentions into architectural language in an accurate and effective manner. The differing personal styles of the teachers and the personalities of each student make this stage unique and unrepeatable; it has to be experienced *face to face* and intensified by shared laboratory team work. The first design plans produced by the student are almost never a coherent or exhaustive expression of his intentions, and a series of questions, answers, objections, suggestions and discussions are needed, which must be carried out in real time for any real didactic exchange to take place. The dialogue has to be tight and emotionally supportive in order to motivate learning, and cannot be diluted or weakened by an exchange of e-mails, for example.

The *telecontiguity* system can resolve the question of naturalness during the real time collaboration stage of design reviewing. The system, under the name of Augmented Whiteboard, is being offered for experimentation because it manages to recreate, in the distance learning area of relationships between teachers, between teachers and students, between universities and external resources, those complex yet normal moments of dialogue which would otherwise be adulterated or altered by the usual e-learning codes and metalanguages. The *telecontiguity* system can be readily integrated into other systems and the success it has achieved in public demonstrations, both with schoolchildren and professional and specialised targets, has made us extremely confident of its usability and the naturalness of its interface.

2. ANTECEDENTS

2.1 Architecture and Communication: since the 19th century, not only a technological challenge

The theme of transferring audiovisual perception, both at a distance and in real time, was already being reported in newspapers and exciting the interest of the public in the last 30 years of the 19th century, from the time the first inventors and experimenters had began to look for names to describe their apparatuses: *electric eye* (C.W. Siemens, 1876), *telephonoscope* (T. Edison, 1879), *telectroscope* and *telephotograph* (C.M. Perosino, 1879).

What we came to call the *telephone* was in actuality the real origin of videoconferencing, in its two-way interactiveness,

3.a
"Thomas Edison's Telephonoscope" cartoon in Punch's Almanack, London 1879.

3.b
"En l'an 2000" French illustration for the science-fiction writer Albert Robida, Paris 1882.

3.c
"Purchase Order at a distance" advertising figurine for Suchard chocolate, Neuchatel, end 19th century.

while television was and still is a derivation, a one-way, non-interactive communication device, despite the experiments in interactive camouflage of recent years. This overcoming of the natural damping factor of distance in space and time (*The Crisis of Modernity*, David Harvey, 1989), immediately attracted the interest of scientists and philosophers, as well as artists and the writers of science-fiction. The three quotations that I have chosen to head this paper bear witness to a fascination with the technological development of video-communication, which was wrongly seen by many as a visionary, prophetic obsession.

The cinema, itself an instrument of communication, primarily and more than any other medium took upon itself an immediate role as a philosophical and scientific laboratory where all the possible evolutions of its destiny as source of architecture and communication could be given expression. This destiny was understood by many film directors, like René Clair when he said: "The art that cinema brings to mind is architecture". In *Metropolis* (F. Lang, 1929), there appears a video-telephone which afterwards became a real public service in certain German post offices for Nazi propaganda of the Berlin Olympics in 1936. The American papers were impressed by these telescreens that transmitted and received at the same time. Eric Blair, better known as George Orwell, a newspaper correspondent at the time, did not see the devices himself but read about them in the international press, and from that point began his obsession with his novel *1984*, which he wanted to publish in 1949, despite being ill with tuberculosis. In the thirties the first experimental television transmissions were already being made, both in the US and in Germany and Italy for the broadcast of Nazi and Fascist propaganda. The early feeling for this common destiny of media and architecture spread into the field of art with the proliferation of artistic manifestos from the intuitions of Futurism to Spatialism (1946-47), where among others the painter and sculptor Carlo Fontana was very active – he would go on to be a consultant in the first experimental RAI transmissions in 1950 – or an architect like Moretti who discussed the impact of the new-born television on the perception of space in his review *Stile* in those same years.

Let us return to the cinema, which from its early days inquired into the concept of interactivity, without any practical outcome, emphasising the invasive and intrusive aspects where eye to eye contact was taken for granted. To cite a couple of famous examples, both influenced by the ideas mentioned earlier, in the version of Orwell's *1984* directed by Radford in 1984, during the morning wake-up call of the protagonist the audiovisual conversation moves from an impersonal insensitive stance to sudden personally directed invective (see also the ear-

4.a-b-c
French sketches for Albert Robida on audiovisual distance communication for domestic, teaching and business purposes, end 19th century.

5.a
The videotelephone in Metropolis by Fritz Lang, 1929.

5.b
The receiving-transmitting screen in the film "1984" by M. Radford, 1984, from the book of the same name by George Orwell, 1949.

5.c
The TV wall in the film "Fahrenheit 451" by F. Truffaut (1966), from the book of the same name by Ray Bradbury, 1953.

6.a-b-c-d
Above: "Telepresence Town Square"
public location in China (Xi'an)
simulation for a CISCO publicity
videoclip – 2008
Below: "Telepresence Town Square"
public location in Italy (Rome)
simulation for a CISCO publicity
videoclip – 2008.

lier BBC version of *1984* directed by Nigel Kneale in 1954). Another interesting example is Ray Bradbury's 1953 novel *Fahrenheit 451*, which was made into a remarkable film by Truffaut in 1966, in which with the use of the TV wall screen, one can already make out an awareness of a need for devices that shift between impersonal dialogue and intimate conversation with the women in their living rooms; here also there is no question that eye contact is taken for granted.

To return to the field of architecture and communication, the explosive nature of their combination managed to dismantle and reconstruct space in a collage that was perfectly realised in the ideas of the Archigram Group in the sixties, and afterwards critically celebrated by Colin Rowe in his article 'Collage City' of 1978. Since then, both postmodernism and deconstructionism have succeeded in formally and conceptually demolishing the idea of the *composition of space*, which has given way to certain definitions which, since 2000 to today, have not yet found a specific domain of reference: *Media Building, Augmented Spaces, Virtual into Real, Invisible Computing, Tangible Media*. This is a clear symptom of a situation already experienced by the *Electric City* at the adoption of the telephone, a device which has not yet entirely lost its destabilising power. This is not the place to examine this outcome in detail, but it was necessary to underline the intimate architectonic and compositional nature of *telecontiguity* and describe its technological antecedents as described above, with the flow of ideas and conceptual expectations without which one could never be able to interpret the origins or the growth or the failure of any invention.

I will end this section on a provocative note with what appears to be an extremely up-to date advertisement for a service offered by a multinational videoconferencing company, Cisco: Telepresence Town Square – 2008. In actual fact, it is still encumbered with the defects of videoconferencing and prudently purports to be a simulation in expectation of real *telecontiguity*.

What might appear to be a paradox, but which demonstrates the laborious progress of international research in the field, even though it is inserted into a Cisco ad (Public Digital Cribb), the experimental network creating this eagerly awaited technological breakthrough is entirely Italian.

2.2 From technological predecessors to the prototype

Both video-telephones and television have sought for a level of realism and naturalness that has never been achieved. Who can forget the delusion we felt as a child when we discovered that the person looking at us from the TV screen was actually looking into the dark lens of a camera, not to mention the mismatching of eye contact and time lag in video-conferences and video-chat.

Videoconferencing in all its versions, from television studio link-ups to the periodical attempts made in both land-line and mobile video-telephones, video-chatting on computers, etc., has always paid the price for being totally unable to satisfy the natural instinct to make eye contact and to approach the screen to reduce the distance between the two interlocutors. This must be the most insidious of the delusions that

from time to time cause the failure of technical solutions providing performances that are objectively innovative but end in being unable to sway the general public. The fact that solutions attempting to astound us meet with so little enthusiasm tends to push the results obtained into the sidelines of specialised applications, and to cause the excitement and interest that are so necessary for continuing research to fade.

If we limit ourselves to the last thirty years and deal with comparable technological systems, without doubt a major event was an artistic experiment called significantly 'Hole in Space': for three nights (11th to 13th November 1980), with no previous build-up, a section of pavement in New York in front of the windows of the Lincoln Center of Performing Arts was audio-visually connected live, at normal scale, to another piece of pavement in Los Angeles in front of a window of the Century City shopping mall. Even here the lack of eye contact is obvious. The reflected ghost in glass and in the mirror is certainly the oldest stratagem used to try to align the direction of sight in false co-presences; a sort of analog chroma-key. There are all sorts of possible versions: from the traditional theatrical effect of *Pepper's Ghost* of 1862, to the video conferences reflected on a simple semi-transparent pane of glass, usually inclined at an angle of 45° over a horizontal monitor. This system allows the camera to be placed behind the glass in front of the participant's eyes, and manages to superimpose his line of sight on to the reflected image of his distant interlocutor. Strange to say, the stratagem used in *Pepper's Ghost* is coming back into vogue in its technologically advanced version, by utilising larger and larger high-definition monitors as well as ever more satisfying performance on the part of digital video-projection. One example will do for all: the heavily publicised (*Telepresence Magic* passed off as a holograph appearing on CNN in 2007) cycle of international conferences on climate that Cisco and Musion created for Al Gore and Prince Charles. If you look closely at the videos on YouTube, it only takes a touch of the freeze frame button on the flashes from the cameras in the theatre to expose the ancient trick. Rather than call it a hologram it would be more honest to dub it 'Pepper's Ghost'.

The reflection on a glass screen inclined at a 45° angle is an effective solution for achieving eye contact at a natural scale, yet it is unsuccessful in that direct contact with the reflection

7.a
First public videotelephone service in the post offices of Nazi Germany 1936-1940.

7.b
AT&T videotelephone at the New York World Fair 1964.

7.c
Hole in Space – 1980 – Link-up New York-Los Angeles – by Kit Galloway and Sherrie Rabinowitz, backed by Western Union, General Electric and World Communications.

8.a-b-c
Hole in Space – 1980 – Link-up New York-Los Angeles (on left) New York (on right) – by Kit Galloway and Sherrie Rabinowitz, backed by Western Union, General Electric and World Communications.

of the ghost cannot be obtained. The reflected image remains suspended on the opposite side to the viewer, and if we were to pass across to the other side, nothing would be seen. So as with the chroma-key we have to make a reflection of ourselves on a monitor or in a mirror where we can see ourselves superimposed on the ghost; a common example of this system can be seen in television weather forecasts where the hand-movements of the presenter on the virtual weather map are obviously unnatural and hesitant precisely because he is forced to check elsewhere the feedback between his hand-movements and the effects of the digital superimposition.

The closest forerunner of telecontiguity for teaching purposes is certainly the *Clear Board* designed by Iroshi Iishi and Minoru Kobayashi (NIT 1992-94). Here the reflected image is projected directly on to the work surface, as can be seen in the diagram. The face to face effect is very close to reality except that when the user's hand or head moves too close to the screen they block the camera's field of view; in this case it becomes impossible, for example, to place on the surface a drawing that is facing towards the distant interlocutor. The brightness quality of the image reflected on the half-mirrored glass screen and of that of the rear-projection is not very high; in fact the effective use of the system and the state of the surrounding lighting depends on there being absolute darkness as a background. The face to face effect is also unbalanced and spread out. Research in this direction was abandoned in 1994 but Minoru Kobayashi (NIT) returned to it in 2003 when he used a somewhat forced artificial perspective in the design of a PC monitor; there was a real-time warping of the videoconference image behind the graphic design.

2.3 The Telecontiguity System prototype and previous experiments

The metaphor of *face to face*, as behind a pane of glass, became real with the first functioning prototype (an internet

9.a
"Pepper's Ghost" the reflection from glass at an inclination of 45° is the invention, for a theatrical effect, of John Henry Pepper professor at the Royal Polytechnic, London, 1862.

9.b
"Telepresence Magic" la version of Pepper's Ghost by Cisco and Musion, revealed in camera flash during a videoconference, 2007.

9.c
"Telepresence Magic" how it appeared to the audience in the darkness of the hall.

10.a-b-c-d-e-f
Photo and operating scheme of the ClearBoard-1 by Hiroshi Iishi and Minoru Kobayashi, NTT Japan 1992 (above) and 1994 (below).

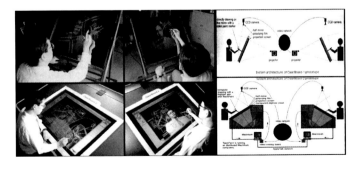

link-up between two positions) presented in public by this writer and his research group, in Campobasso, on March 17th, 2006, in the Università degli Studi del Molise, during the XVI Scientific and Technological Culture Week of the Ministry of Education, Universities and Research (MIUR).

Previous experiments in public with similar equipment that was not truly telecontiguous had been carried out in Milan, Venice and Rome. Our research had attracted the attention of and contributions from Cinecittà, the RAI, Ericsson Telecommunications, 3M, Studio Azzurro, the Rome Association of Architects, the Artistic Heritage Department of Rome City Council, the Architecture Biennale of Venice and Beijing and professionals and companies involved in innovative communication in the arts, in advertising and broadcasting.

The three main experiments were:

Menopossibile – videoclip, 2001. Concept for the International competition Video in Architecture "Beyond Media" Florence, 2 May, 2001

Stefano Panunzi (author), Gianluca Adami (direction), Alessandro Santamaria Ferraro (montage and postproduction).

Successively redesigned with the title '1.0. W.A.L.L.' an acronym of Web Amplified Life on Line (pixels/m^2 – 283.460) for a project chosen for the international competition on the theme of the Virtual Museum organized by NewItalian-Blood.com – 2001.

The 'Display Room' was imagined for a house whose walls were entirely made up of screens. An electronic transparency creates digital barriers, re-modelling the space according to its significance and the chosen bi-directional connections, to link separate rooms together and apportion virtual links between real spaces at a distance.

Master in Design of Interactive Spaces for Communication, 2002

ICT Laboratory of the Department of architectural and Urban Design of the Sapienza University of Rome.

Stefano Panunzi STAFF: Gianluca Adami, Alessandro Santamaria, Onorino Proietti. In the photo, the architects enrolled in the Master course: Lucia Frasca Polara, Salvatore Marinaro, Maddalena Cannarsa.

NEXT 2002 – International Architecture Biennale of Venice and PiazzaNavona@SMAU, 2002
Public experiment with link-up between the Teatro dell'Arsenale (Venice) and the window of Palazzo Lancellotti overlooking Piazza Navona.

The experiment was repeated under the title *PiazzaNavona@SMAU* linking the piazza with the Ericsson Telecommunication stand for SMAU 2002 in Milan. In Octo-

11.a-b-c
Touching the same point on the glass with the index finger of the right hand and the toast between two glasses during the first public demonstration of the telecontiguity prototype, March 2006. Stefano Panunzi with the technical collaboration of Mario Petrone, Roberto Zarrelli, Angelo Iannaccio, Eugenio Pasquariello and Andrea Campidoglio of the Università degli Studi del Molise Information Science Laborator.

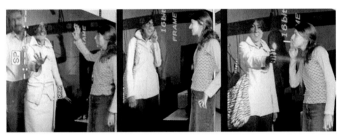

ber 2004 it was presented at the International Architecture Biennale of Beijing.

Stefano Panunzi (author) STAFF: Tiziana Barcaroli, Samantha Emanuele, Livia Cannella, Alessandro Santamaria, Gianluca Adami, Onorino Proietti.

3. RESEARCH REPORT: PRIN 2006 AND SCIENTIFIC NETWORK FOR TELECONTIGUITY SYSTEM EXPERIMENTATION

3.1 The telecontiguity system and remote synchronous collaboration

The basic system comprises terminals equipped with hardware and software for:
- audio and video data transmission in High Definition on
- IP protocol
- real time digital image processing
- treatment and special applications of glass surfaces
- special lighting
- interactive wireless peripherals

The Molise Research Unit, during the experiments, created:
- a fixed position inside the Computer Technology Room at Termoli University, with the entire system enclosed in a technically-equipped environment, leaving open towards the room only the glass surface to be used for the interactions
- a mobile position (screen and trolley) as a terminal for the distance dialogue

12.a-b-c
"Menopossibile" (Lesspossibile)
videoclip – 2001 (Concept of
Telecontiguity).

13.a-b-c
"Design of Interactive Spaces for
Communication" post-graduate
Masters degree for architects. January
2002 (off-line simulation).

14.a-b-c
Venice International Biennale of
Architecture "NEXT 2002"
October 2002 (ISDN Venice-Rome and
Milan-Rome).

This second solution appeared necessary after various types of set up had been tested. The aim was to understand the vulnerability inherent in the optimal use conditions, above all the features of the user base (colours and room lighting).

After the analytical testing stage of the performative states, restricted to various alternative solutions for the screens, we considered we could justify investment in High Definition and Dual Video videoconference apparatus, as well as a real time digital manipulation Mixer. The optimal solution for the screens was obtained after the final public experiment (at the World Congress on Architecture UIA 2008 at the Lingotto, Turin, July 2008).

As from the 2nd year, various research fronts opened up for us to obtain our final objective of usability for distance learning, passing over to HD videoconferencing data transmission. A basic apparatus for the first test was acquired along with its twin from the Rome Unit, which had had great success and which gave us the opportunity to equip each campus of the Università degli Studi del Molise with its own HD terminal (one in the central campus of Campobasso and in the three campuses of Isernia-Pesche-Termoli.)

Experimenting with a real-time mixage system with standard HD for the superimposition in croma-key of the desk-top graphics on the videoconferencing transmission. For this purpose a mixer console for HD was acquired (also for the Rome Unit) which was capable of bearing the signal in Dual Video (double transmission channel: video-camera and PC desktop) carried from the videoconferencing apparatus.

Feasibility of auto-collimation systems in the two triads telecamera-video-projector-screen intersected at a distance by the two connected terminals. Reciprocal manual matching between the capture frame and projection frame was a crucial problem, complicated by the high number of optical variables in play in the set up of the terminals and the resetting every time they were switched on or off. The possibility of an automatic matching system was resolved by resorting to algorithmic programming, and this was carried out by a physicist appointed to the contract who is an expert in artificial vision, Dr Giovanni Avanzi. The specific topic of his research activity was "the feasibility analysis of hardware and software solutions for the automatic calibration of digital broadcasting in videoconferencing" (Dip. SAVA 24-09-08). At the end of the contract a first software and hardware package was developed which could be adapted for the automatic collimation of the system.

Feasibility of interactive wireless peripherals compatible with any type of software application (CAD, research

15.a
Window constructed for permanent installation of telecontiguity glass screen, facing into the Information Science Room of the Termoli campus of the Università degli Studi del Molise. The entire system of projection/filming/mixage/transmission was installed on the premises.

15.b
Test of the overprinting of the desktop graphics in link-up with Rome (using mobile whiteboard).

15.c
The transparent mobile whiteboard, when not in use as a screen for the telecontiguity.

16.a
Trolley for the mobile unit of the telecontiguity system, working design by Mario De Lucrezia (in the photo) thanks to the convention with the Trento Development Agency.

16.b
All the basic apparatus needed is pre-installed inside; a system of pantographs automatically put into position all the components of the system.

16.c
Augmented Whiteboard. The whiteboard, which can be adjusted in height, is equipped with its own adjustable lighting system.

17.a
The Dual Video HD videoconference system can enlarge and send the remote desktop on the window on one channel, so that it physically interacts on the graphics and is filmed in videoconference on the other channel.

17.b
Testing the feasibility of a design review session at a distance between several people in front of the screen at the same time.

17.c
The desktop of the teacher's or the student's laptop which sends the graphical image to be reviewed on the window shared in telecontiguity.

engines, etc.) The recent developments in wireless peripherals for playstations and the deregulation of software for development gave us the idea of handing over this kind of programming to a specialist to see if it was possible to use this sort of interaction on the telecontiguity surface. We therefore contracted the programming expert Daniele Pellegrini for "the feasibility analysis of hardware and software solutions for shared interactivity on 3D models in video-conferencing" (Dip. SAVA 24-09-08). Also in this case there was shown to be a perfect feasibility of programming plug-ins for any type of application (from CAD software to internet applications) which could exercise control by means of the most common playstation peripherals. Two playstations were acquired along with their peripherals (Wii Nintendo) and a third with a higher processing potential (Playstation 3).

3.2 Application development and patent

The Telecontiguity System, thanks to this funding, has reached the level of usability that was pre-established for it. The principal modules of the system can therefore be inaugurated into the pre-industrial research phase, for the purpose of acquiring specific patentable procedures and spin-off applications:

A telecontiguity screen (Augmented Window) overprinted with any application from the desktop of the user's PC (Augmented Desktop)

The system can be equipped with automatic matching between the capture frame and the projection frame with continuous feedback from the installation for the entire duration of the link ups.

The system can be equipped with interactive wireless peripherals compatible with the most common applications.

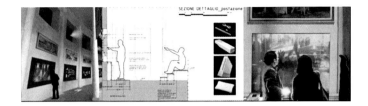

3.3 Experimental demonstrations and the partners of the Scientific Network of Experimentation of the Telecontiguity System

On the experimental front we have found it necessary to combine the research applied to the system with the remote terminals and laboratories that were already active before the PRIN 2006 funding. The research contracts were therefore able to avail themselves of already existing experimental infrastructures, especially those of the Development Agency of Trento and the Association of Architects:
- The Trento Agency for the development of the portability of the system (Mario Di Lucrezia)
- The Architects Association for the interaction with virtual models (Daniele Pellegrini)

In order to examine the naturalness of use of the system as its strongest feature, in situations open to a varied public, without any kind of specialised function, we created public occasions where the entire system was hidden and protected behind the screen and was accessible only to those in charge of the research and to authorised technicians, for obvious patenting reasons. The public had only the surface in plexiglass or glass (which was specially treated according to the differing occasions), soluble marker pens, sheets of paper and faxes from one side to the other.

The contact with the public was considered to be necessary during the whole stage of experiments involving the replacement of materials and treatments used for the screens. Until we had achieved satisfactory results it would have been of little use making any investment in technological video-transmission instruments for the layout of graphics for interactive sharing. Given the different research competences of the other units involved in the PRIN research, The Molise Research Unit experiments from the start needed to find partners who could afford an investment for the experiments with the wide-spectrum terminal.

For this reason conventions[5] for the Telecontiguity System experimentation were made with the Trento Development Agency and the Rome Association of Architects. With the Trento Agency the agreement was above all for a scholarship for the working design of a portable system, and with the Association the organisation of experimental events involving the general public. The first of these events coincided with the actual start of the PRIN research.

Build Up Expo 6-10 February 2007
(Rome Aquarium – Milan New Fair)
The two places connected were the Build-Up Expo at the

18.a-b-c-d
Study of the sensors and periphericals for complex 3D interactions on the screen; dissertation project of Emanuele Sinisi, supervisor Stefano Panunzi, developed for the Convention with the Rome Architects Association.

New Fair of Milan, and the Rome Aquarium (Home of Architecture), seat of the Architects' Association PPC of the city and province of Rome. In this event, the system was set up according to two completely different principles: in Milan, there was a sheet of plexi-glass attached to the ceiling and the rest of the system hidden behind a black wall further back from the screen. The Milan location was a Hi-Tech stand of the Architects' Association dominated by reflections and gaudy light shows. The screen in the Rome Aquarium on the other hand completely closed off an aperture in the historic building, in a warmer atmosphere with soft lighting and neo-classical decoration. Beneath each screen was a table with glass screen marker pens, an eraser and a fax machine. The audio element involved speakers and omni-directional microphones. The link-up lasted 4 days from 9 in the morning until 6 pm. The experiment was also reported in the national press (Il Sole 24 Ore, insert 'NOVA').

17th Week of Culture Science and Technology, MIUR 23 March 2007
(Rome Aquarium – Faculty of Engineering, Termoli)
The two linked locations were the Conference Hall of the Termoli campus (Engineering-Economics) of the Università degli Studi del Molise, and the Rome Aquarium. The set up at the Aquarium was the same as that of the previous Build Up Expo event, while in the Conference Hall a simple table was set up with the screen fixed to it by tie-rods. The object of the experiment was to describe degree dissertations from Rome to the audience in Termoli. The author interacted from Termoli with the Roman students in the Aquarium, using exclusively variously coloured glass screen marker pens.

BIC Day of the Trento District Development Agency, Rovereto, 5 December 2007
(Trento District Development Agency – Computer Laboratory of the Università degli Studi del Molise at Campobasso)
This link-up was the first open to the general public, with another telecontiguity terminal set up in the Development Agency's headquarters, fixed to a frame and visible to all those present. The link-up was used mainly for group inter-

19.a-b-c
Build Up Expò 6 – 10 February 2007
(Roma Aquarium – Milano New Fair).

20.a-b-c
XVII Scientific and Technological
Culture Week, MIUR 23 March 2007
(Roma Aquarium – Faculty of
Engineering, Termoli).

actions, to see how natural an informal discussion could be without any order to the interventions, and to check the dynamics of eye contact during the dialogues, and to identify the interlocutors who interrupted or asked to speak. The only negative point was the delay in transmission in the cut and thrust of the exchanges, while the sub-optimal quality of the image was compensated for by the excellent sound quality. A simple omni-directional microphone was used in both locations.

UIA Turin 29 June-3 July 2008
The Lingotto of Turin – Rome Aquarium – Trento Development Agency – Engineering Faculty, Termoli)
At the World Conference on Architecture, held in the Lingotto of Turin from June 29 to July 3, 2009, the Architects' Association PPC of the city and province of Rome entrusted the author with the scientific supervision of the setting up of the stand. The project involved different forms of distance communication: the telecontiguity screen for the link-up with the Association's seat in the Rome Aquarium, equipped for the occasion with an anti-dazzle visor, large LCD screens to test the video resolution of a link-up with a lap-top from Arcosanti (Arizona) connected via Skype, link-ups between cell phones (H3G) with Skype keys and remote desktops to be shown on the telecontiguity screen (this last experiment failed to work since there was found to be a disparity in the two protocols, between cell phone and lap-top).

21.a-b-c
BIC Day of the Trento Development Agency, Rovereto, 5 December 2007 (Trento Development Agency – Computer Lab Università degli Studi del Molise Campobasso)
The permanent installation for the Trento Development Agency, research partners.

22.a-b-c
Test for group discussion at the BIC Day in Trento in link-up with the mobile location installed in the Computer Lab Università degli Studi del Molise, Campobasso.

23.a
The telecontiguity screen on the Rome Architects Association stand ay the World Architecture Congress UIA 2008 at the Lingotto, Torino.

23.b
The link-up with the Rome Aquarium Headquarters of the Association).

23.c
Collimation tests of the telecontiguity window between Roberto Vacca (Roma) and Stefano Panunzi (Torino).

NOTES

[1] The neologism *telecontiguity* is literally a contradiction in terms, referring to the possibility of making two distant spaces appear to be adjacent to one another, as if they were separated by a pane of glass; the image is tele-transmitted at actual scale and is produced by a fixed camera. The innovation of the system lies in the reciprocal correspondence between the frame of the projected image and that of the filmed image, forming a real surface of reciprocal contact, which at the present stage, can be as large as the wall of a room.

[2] Research into new teaching technologies began in 1986 at the International eCAADe Conference 'Teaching and Research Experience with CAAD'. Since 1989 it has been officially funded

(Ministry of Education Research coordinated by Prof. Paola Coppola) Production of Multimedia Circuits for Teaching purposes, and continued from 2000 to 2004 in a European WINDS project coordinated by Prof. Mario De Grassi, and reached its first experimental stages in 2000 (Master in design of Interactive Spaces for Communication, created and coordinated by S.Panunzi and directed by Prof. Lucio Valerio Barbera), and tested on a first working prototype in 2006,. Since then the research has entered a stage of technological upgrading with applied experimentation, also thanks to timely funding by PRIN 2006 and from this year has been used in various experimental start-ups in different application environments (H3G SpA, Rome Architects' Association and the Trento Development Agency).

[3] The most similar cases:

A) Clearboard 1 e 2 by Hiroshi Ishii, Minoru Kobayashi, NTT Human Interface Laboratories, Japan 1992

B) Interactive Video System British Telecommunications 2005, International patent refused

[4] Edward T.Hall, founder of proxemics (1963) the discipline which studies the space and distances inside a communicative act, both verbal and non-verbal. In classifying various cases, the critical distance between teacher and student goes from a minimum of 1.2 m. to 3,5m, which in a videoconferencing situation can be divided in half for each side, 60 cm and 1, 75 cm. In *telecontiguity* the minimum distance of 60 cm. is practicable in face to face interactions at a 1: 1 scale, with eye contact and touchability of the screen.

[5] 2007/2009 two-year agreement with *Parco Tecnologico – Agenzia Sviluppo Trentino spa*

2007/2009 two-year agreement with *Ordine degli Architetti PPC di Roma e Provincia*

2008/2011 three-year agreement with *H3G spa (mobile telephones3)*

Chronological Record (1986-2009)

1986 TEACHING AND RESEARCH EXPERIENCE WITH CAAD

Panunzi, Stefano and Sansoni, Claudio (1986) Transformations of the Shanberg House – Analysis of a Plan and Planning Experimentations, Using the Instruments of Multi-criteria Analysis as Means of Research., [4th eCAADe Conference Proceedings] Rome (Italy) 11-13 September 1986, pp. 97-110

1986-1990 RESEARCH DOCTORATE IN ARCHITECTURAL COMPOSITION, SAPIENZA UNIVERSITÀ DI ROMA-SOILS, ENCLOSURES, THRESHOLDS, COVERINGS Stefano Panunzi

Quaderni del Dottorato di Ricerca in Composizione Architettonica

Dipartimento di Progettazione Architettonica e Urbana

Dipartimento di Architettura e Analisi della Città

University of Rome "La Sapienza" – Gangemi, 1994

We need to think about the web of meanings that exist between the space of connection and the edges open to other spaces (the architecture of connection of Louis Khan). These places are above all places of looking: you look at where you are going and what you are going through, at who is coming and who is passing by, your eyes meet the eyes of the others, the glimpses caught at the opening edges. It is an 'Ariadne's thread' for anyone searching for sense in that 'virtual' reality where very soon we shall all have to interact and come up with ideas that are far more lucid than any we have entertained so far.

1989-1992 INTER-UNIVERSITY SCIENTIFIC RESEARCH "THE PRODUCTION OF MULTIMEDIA CIRCUITS" TRASCRIBING TIME INTO ARCHITECTONIC SPACE Stefano Panunzi

Animated Image and Architectural Representation IMARA '93 – Montecarlo – Conference 16-19 February 1993 published in Italy in *Archimedia* n°1 Jan-Feb 1994, MGE Communications

INTER-UNIVERSITY SCIENTIFIC RESEARCH "The production of didactic multimedia circuits for architecture and town planning" (Architecture Faculties of Paris, Bordeaux, Venice, Milan, Florence, Rome 1989-92)

The tele-vision of architecture is literally an electronic communication of space uttered by time. In this case the communication has to be created by the syntax of architectonic language. Architecture is not a text to be read but a voice to be listened to. We have to be able to give voice to the language of architecture and at the same time enable it to be heard. The traditional rules of cinema and television filming establish various relations with the space that is filmed and give birth to different kinds of communicative figures: the fixed camera designates the event. Architecture as a fixed scene for an event or a phenomenon. The communicative figure of the event gives voice to all the architectonic elements that accept, contain and permit live events and phenomena to happen. In a fixed shot of a place all the information is present on the scene; it can only be augmented by dynamic events and phenomena that take place during the shooting. The fixed scene sets up the expectancy and absorbs the dynamic time of the event.

1996 IN VOLO SULLA CITTÀ (FLYING OVER THE CITY) Multimedia interactive atlas of the city of Rome, with Roberto Cera e Andrea Flego.

1998 FOUNDATION OF LaMA, Laboratorio Multimediale di Architettura – Dipartimento di Progettazione Architettonica e Urbana, University of Rome 'La Sapienza'.

1998-2002 WINDS (2000-2003)
WEB BASED INTELLIGENT DESIGN TUTORING SYSTEM (FIFTH FRAME-
WORK PROGRAMME UE–IST INFORMATION SOCIETY TECHNOLOGY)

2000 ARCHITECTURE AND COMMUNICATION – INTERNATIONAL
CONFERENCE, Università degli Studi La Sapienza di Roma.

2000 JOURNEYS THROUGH THE CITY OF THE THIRD MILLENIUM –
BNL INVESTMENTS

2001 INTERNATIONAL COMPETITION NEWITALIANBLOOD "VIRTUAL
MUSEUM"
W.A.L.L. WEB AMPLIFIED LIFE ON-LINE (MAY 2001 VIDEO 3'20")
Stefano Panunzi (author), Alessandro Santamaria (postpro-
duction), Gianluca Adami (direction) (May 2001 – video 3'20")

2001 LESS POSSIBLE (revised version of November 2001 after
the fall of the Twin Towers 9/11) Presented at the *Rassegna In-
ternazionale Beyond Media – oltre i media, architettura in video*.
Catalogue of International architecture meetings – Editrice
Compositori – Florence 2/5 May 2002
*"Our houses will be stripped of useless accretions that obstruct the
space, in order to provide as many surfaces as possible to be smeared
with images and digital sounds which via the web will link us to other places, other people and other emotions. A digital telecontiguity will
be created between real spaces transforming walls into interfaces,
something that the poetry of mature visionaries foresaw long ago"*

2002 VENICE INTERNATIONAL ARCHITECTURE BIENNALE NEXT 2002
*Architettura come interfaccia: Porte della Percezione & Ambi-
enti Sensibili.*
Stefano Panunzi (design and coordination) Conference-Event
International Architecture Biennale NEXT – Teatro delle
Tese all'Arsenale – Venice 19 October 2002
Master in Design of Interactive Spaces for Communication
Department of Architectural and Urban Design, of Land-
scape and Interiors, Rome University "La Sapienza" sponsored
by the Rome Architects Association, RAI TV Production Divi-
sion, Ericsson Telecommunications, Studio Azzurro
*"Transmission tests in tele-contiguity with Piazza Navona and
Naples (Castel Sant'Elmo) for the inauguration of the installation
"Mediterranean Meditation" of Studio Azzurro, display of construction site of the 'navigable city' with its conceptual, material and technological experiments. The aim of the experimentation carried out was
to integrate a moving cell phone user with large digital surfaces set up
in both internal and external urban spaces (shop windows, billboards,
building facades). Squares, display areas, places where people wait or
rest, archaeological sites are remodelled into spaces that are sensitive
to the presence of the users, that can provide a real broadcast of events
and facilities which can be shaped to order in space and time. The cell
phone has been experimentally transformed into a universal pointer
which everyone can use: with the keyboard you can move the cursor,
click and type letters from the keyboard directly on to the interactive
surfaces that we come across on our daily travels. The possible facilities can be those normally available on the net, on television programmes, on local information networks, plus an infinite number of
new possibilities that will have to adapt themselves to this new form*

of resource in the shape of large-scale displays and users moving through the city. Telecontiguity is the scientific term, coined for the occasion, which best sums up this revolutionary way of utilising architectonic and urban space tank to new information and communication technologies. The complementary nature of the fixed and mobile nets is demonstrated by means of applications which separate the video facility from that of the voice. The cell phone identifies the person, allowing him to communicate and interact with the world around him; it will allow him to access services that are 'carved out' and 'activated' by his own presence in a given environment".

2002 SMAU Milano "Piazza Navona @ SMAU"
Stefano Panunzi (design e coordination) event in telecontiguity connecting a window of Palazzo Lancillotti in Piazza Navona and the Ericsson Stand at the SMAU of Milan – October 2002

2003 Exhibition at the Casa dell'Architettura in Rome "Trials for an imminent city"
Stefano Panunzi (curator) exhibition at the Rome Aquarium – Casa dell'Architettura 28/29 March 2003 – in AR Bimestrale dell'Ordine degli Architetti di Roma e Provincia – n.47 May/June 2003
Telecontiguity and interactivity *are inherent qualities of the Electric City of the 20th century, which remained hidden and disguised in the chrysalis of the nineteenth century city. Digital convergence has now made it easier for us to visualise the radical transformations that began with the electrification of cities*
Augmented Perceptions: *our natural perceptions are augmented and condensed around the communication portals (telephone-radio-television-internet).*
Sensitive spaces: *real space has invisibly become increasingly sensitive to whoever lives in it and moves through it (tele-surveillance-super-vision, satellite cards, code-password-net, cell phone)* Convergence: *these two processes, until now parallel to one another are being fused through interactivity. The social impact of these changes will not only be linked to the cost of access (purchase of terminals and duties on traffic) but will depend on their capacity to be used by everyone, everywhere, in a natural way, and on their ability to bring closer and render accessible in time and space living realities, and make invisible realities visible.*
The architectural and urban scene as a communicative interface: *From maxi-screens to LEDs and high-resolution and high-luminosity video projections, digital imagery has now assumed formats that are extendable, modular and projective, and which can correspond to components of the lexicon of architecture: windows, walls, facades. These architectonic surfaces will become communicative interfaces that can be controller by moving users with cell phones and/or third-generation palm-tops. Services and personalised events will be activated by the simple presence of a user in the interactive architectonic urban space; the quality and number of presences will be registered in real time by sensors, by the Geographical Positioning System (GPS) or by the mobile phone radio-link cells.*
New parameters of space and communication: time, surfaces and position: *the walls, windows, facades, both real and interactive, will have an economic value measured in square metres multiplied by the seconds of transmission, the number of real users present in the space and the number of virtual contacts arriving from the net. All the services offered by the net can be directed on to this surface-interface, as well as those of web-TV, web-cinema, etc. The only difficulty is how to explain clearly to the ordinary mass consumer the real innovative power of these sce-*

narios. On the other hand, spot-architecture and media– building already embody the latest version of a fusion between communication and architecture that had been developing throughout the 20th century.

After 'virtual'reality, the time has come for experimenting with virtuality within reality: *the architect, along with many other professional figures, is called upon to invent, compose and set up scenarios for the telecontiguity and stereo-reality of real physical space. The convergence of media on the cell phone-internet will mean more dialogue with real space in a hybrid condition of virtual-within-real, which today we can only try to imagine, and which should create a genuine conception of interactivity, based on our natural interfaces.*

2004 RESEARCH AND PROJECT NOTES – REFLECTIONS ON CONTEMPORARY HOUSING "NEXT HOUSING"

Stefano Panunzi in *Riflessioni sull'abitazione contemporanea* – Quaderno di Ricerca e Progetto, Dipartimento di Progettazione Architettonica e Urbana del Paesaggio e degli Interni

University of Rome "La Sapienza" – Gangemi Editore – 2004

Installations (archi-network): *The accepted meaning of installation is now that best applied to define contemporary architecture, a real transformation of architectonic coverings into interfaces for ecological and communication networks. (…) The speed of connectivity of the information-mobile nets have immersed us in a real digital amniotic fluid that can be genetically remodelled, utterly transforming the image of the planet into a genuine global womb.*

Furnishing (display furniture): *Furnishings retain their role in describing places, and consign it to the digital image that conforms to it. The concept of scene and backdrop has become a common idea in the theatre of everyday life. Furniture, apart from its indispensible uses, provides surfaces that can be used for video-projection: wardrobe doors, curtains, pictures, walls, or doorframes can all be treated with reflecting paint so as to heighten the digital luminosity; cornices, mouldings, colours and ornamental elements, door knobs, handles and keys will be eliminated; everything should be minimal, smooth and uniform. The wealthiest cover everything using Cambridge Display Technology (CDT, a polymer sheet with an active matrix) others content themselves with video-projections where the depth of field allows for the appropriate size of frame.*

Facades (screen walls): *Existing building facades have almost all been covered in screens and glass plates. Polarised glass that becomes opaque when necessary, electro-luminescent, transparent, filtering the light (…) This mother pearl veneer is further enhanced by a mosaic of sparkling LED-walls inserts that remain lit during the day and are applied to the reflecting walls.*

Windows (electronic prospects): *Windows have always had a double implication: facing from the inside towards the outside, and being empty holes in a building viewed from the outside. Today some windows are true electronic openings from a real interior towards a telecontiguous exterior Electronic transparency has been added to the familiar functions to which glass and mirrors have accustomed us, transparency and the reflection of our surroundings (here) which are today located in the tele-contiguous (elsewhere).*

Walls (screen walls): *the entire wall surface can accommodate a digital image. This fact has reduced to a minimum any interference that could affect the viewing of the digital image (see furnishings). Looking at the walls of an apartment, one can understand the tenor of its occupants' lives. Entirely hardwired with polymeric active matrices, or with reflecting materials to ensure the most economical video-pro-*

jection. Everywhere today digital images are tele-visions, attached to us like our shadows, following us by sliding from one surface to another.

Doors (doors of perception): *Alongside the normal doors in our houses there are "doors of perception". These doors open and close, but only our perceptions, not our bodies, cross their thresholds. Seen from this viewpoint, we have always lived with this kind of door: pictures on our walls, television, radio, telephones, photographs and decorations, all reclassified as doors of perception.*

2004 Third Williams Symposium on Classical Architecture "Il virtuale nel reale: il caso del Foro di Augusto", American Academy in Rome, the British School at Rome and the Deutsches Archäologisches Institut, Rome, on May 20-23, Claudia Cecamore, Lucrezia Ungaro & Stefano Panunzi.
Imaging Ancient Rome Documentation – Visualization – Imagination.
Journal of Roman Archaeology Supplementary Series Number 61.

2005 Palindroma: la città degli angeli (the city of the angels) (architecture and multimediality).
Panunzi S. (2005). in *METAMORFOSI*. vol. 55 pp. 54-57 ISSN: 1590-1394.
The article deals with the transformation of architectural and urban space with 'telecontiguity' systems, interactive communication between places at a distance by means of the sharing of audiovisual and tactile surfaces.

2006 the Frontiers of Architecture: Paola Coppola Pignatelli Scritti-Progetti-Ricerche 1950-2005 by Stefano Panunzi, with Domizia Mandolesi and Rosalba Belibani, (Rome 2006).
"There is no getting away from it: weaving space and time together is the task of demigods. For this reason fearful architects hide themselves away in history or in technique, avoiding the confrontation and renouncing any search for the key that connects the unfolding of time with the non-temporality of mankind" (Paola Coppola Pignatelli "Durezza dell'Ars Aedificandi" in "Tempo e Architettura" Gangemi 1987.
By now all of time is flowing into space and is becoming usable as a place, all we have to do is wander freely through it back and forth, and add new chapters to history. In this time that has become space, telecontiguity has brought about chrono-contiguity, in that the obstacle of distance is now almost non-existent and no longer produces time, the time that separates and consumes existence in space. The beginning of a palindromic tale is also its end.

2008 Agir pour la ville e le territorie (29/5/2008).
Salon de la Cité: first Franco-Italian meeting in the Casa dell'Architettura (Rome Aquarium) Rome
"We will park on the roofs, under hanging gardens connected one to another, while above run the urban cableways and below rooms encounter each other in telecontiguity. But these are the first prototypes of Urban Reverse Engineering on which we will reach agreement in the Salon de la Cité…".

2009 100 years after Futurism, what future for Rome and Paris? (22/5 /2009)
Salon de la Cité: second Franco-Italian meeting in the Casa dell'Architettura (Rome Aquarium) Rome. *A project was presented for a telecontiguity link-up between Rome and Paris.*

BIBLIOGRAPHY

TELEPRESENCE

Edouard Lamboray, Stephan Wurmlin, Markus Gross, "Data Streaming in Telepresence Environments", *j-IEEE-TRANS-VIS-COMPUT-GRAPH*, 11 (6), pp. 637-348, November /December 2005.

J. Mulligan, X. Zabulis, N. Kelshikar, K. Daniilidis, "Stereo-based environment scanning for immersive telepresence", *j-IEEE Trans. Circuits and Systems for Video Technology*, 14 (3), pp. 304-320, March 2004.

B. J. Lei, C. Chang, E. A. Hendriks, "An efficient image-based telepresence system for videoconferencing", *IEEE Trans. Circuits and Systems for Video Technology*, 14 (3), pp. 335-347, March 2004.

Henry Fuchs, "Immersive Integration of Physical and Virtual Environments", *Computer Graphics Forum*, 23 (3), pp. 268-268, The Eurographics Association and Blackwell Publishing Ltd, 2004.

S. Ikeda, T. Sato, M. Kanbara, N. Yokoya, *An immersive telepresence system with a locomotion interface using high-resolution omnidirectional movies*, International Conference on Pattern Recognition, p. IV: 396-399, 2004.

Markus Gross, Stephan Würmlin, Martin Naef, Edouard Lamboray, Christian Spagno, Andreas Kunz, Esther Koller-Meier, Tomas Svoboda, Luc Van Gool, Silke Lang, Kai Strehlke, Oliver Staadt, "blue-c: a spatially immersive display and 3D video portal for telepresence", *Proceedings of ACM SIGGRAPH* 2003, ACM Transactions on Graphics, Vol. 22 (3), pp. 819-827, 2003.

S. Ikeda, T. Sato, N. Yokoya, "Panoramic Movie Generation Using an Omnidirectional Multi-camera System for Telepresence", *Scandinavian Conference on Image Analysis*, pp. 1074-1081, 2003.

AUGMENTED REALITY

S. Dasgupta, A. Banerjee, "An Augmented-Reality-Based Real-Time Panoramic Vision System for Autonomous Navigation", *SMC-A*, 36 (1), pp. 154-161, January 2006.

H. Park, M. H. Lee, S. J. Kim, J. I. Park, *Surface-Independent Direct-Projected Augmented Reality*, Asian Conference on Computer Vision, p. II: 892-901, 2006.

A. del Río, J. Fischer, M. Köbele, D. Bartz, W. Straßer, "Augmented Reality Interaction for Semiautomatic Volume Classification", *9th Int. Workshop on Immersive Projection Technology, 11th Eurographics Workshop on Virtual Environments*, pp. 113-120, Eurographics Association, 2005.

Dongdong Weng, Yongtian Wang, Yue Liu, "Applications of Augmented Reality for Maintenance Training", *9th Int. Workshop on Immersive Projection Technology, 11th Eurographics Workshop on Virtual Environments*, pp. 219-220, Eurographics Association, 2005.

Mark A. Livingston, "Evaluating Human Factors in Augmented Reality Systems", *j-IEEE-CGA, 25 (6)*, pp. 6-9, November /December 2005.

Holger Regenbrecht, Gregory Baratoff, Wilhelm Wilke, "Augmented Reality Projects in the Automotive – Aerospace Industries", *j-IEEE-CGA*, 25 (6), pp. 48-56, November /December 2005.

Andreas Oppermann, "Augmented Reality Autorenumgebung – Ein System zur Erstellung von Prozessabläufen mit VR-Inhalten", *BibTeX*, Publications of the Department of Simulation and Graphics at the Otto-von-Guericke University Magdeburg, Germany, February 2005.

T. Kakuta, T. Oishi, K. Ikeuchi, "Virtual Kawaradera: Fast Shadow Texture for Augmented Reality", *CREST05*, pp. 79-85, 2005.

E. Rosten – G. Reitmayr – T. Drummond, "Real-Time Video Annotations for Augmented Reality", *Advances in Visual Computing*, pp. 294-302, 2005.

B. Boufama, A. Habed, "Registration and Tracking In the Context of Augmented Reality", *Graphics, Vision and Image Processing*, Vol. 05, Number V3, p. xx-yy, 2005.

C. Yuan, "Visual Tracking for Seamless 3D Interactions in Augmented Reality", *Advances in Visual Computing*, pp. 321-328, 2005.

L. F. B. Lopes, A. C. Sementille, J. R. F. Brega, F. L. S. N. Marques, I. A. Rodello, "ARISupport: Interaction Support for Augmented Reality Systems" – *Advances in Visual Computing*, pp. 329-336, 2005.

A. Dell'Acqua, M. Ferrari, M. Marcon, A. Sarti, S. Tubaro, "Colored visual tags: a robust approach for augmented reality" – *Advanced Video and Signal Based Surveillance*, pp. 423-427, 2005.

D. J. Johnston, M. Fleury, A. C. Downton, A. F. Clark, "Real-time positioning for augmented reality on a custom parallel machine" – *Image and Vision Computing*, 23 (3), pp. 271-286, March 2005.

A. M. Demiris, V. Vlahakis, A. Makri, M. Papaioannou, N. Ioannidis – "intGuide: A platform for context-aware services featuring augmented-reality, based on the outcome of European Research Projects", *SP: IC*, Vol. 20, Number 9-10, pp. 927-946, October 2005.

Blair MacIntyre, Maribeth G-y, Steven Dow, Jay David Bolter, *DART:* "a toolkit for rapid design exploration of augmented reality experiences", *j-TOG*, 24 (3), pp. 932-932, July 2005.

Mark Billinghurst, Raphael Grasset, Julian Looser, "Designing augmented reality interfaces", *j-COMP-GRAPHICS*, 39 (1), pp. 17-22, February 2005.

M. L. Yuan, S. K. Ong, A. Y. C. Nee, "Registration Based on Projective Reconstruction Technique for Augmented Reality Systems", *j-IEEE-TRANS-VIS-COMPUT-GRAPH*, 11 (3), pp. 254-264, May /June 2005.

Grigore C. Burdea, Ming C. Lin, William Ribarsky, Benjamin Watson, "Guest Editorial: Special Issue on Haptics, Virtual, and Augmented Reality", *j-IEEE-TRANS-VIS-COMPUT-GRAPH*, 11 (6), pp. 611-613, November /December 2005.

Wolfgang Broll-Irma, Lindt-Jan, Ohlenburg-Iris, Herbst-Michael Wittkamper, Thomas Novotny, "An Infrastructure for Realizing Custom-Tailored Augmented Reality User Interfaces", *j-IEEE-TRANS-VIS-COMPUT-GRAPH*, 11 (6), pp. 722-733, November /December 2005.

Paul Benölken, Holger Graf, André Stark, "Texture Based Flow Visualization in Augmented and Virtual Reality Environments", *Journal of WSCG*, Vol. 12, UNION Agency – Science Press, February 2004.

Bernd Schwald, Helmut Seibert, "Registration Tasks for a Hybrid Tracking System for Medical Augmented Reality", *Journal of WSCG*, Vol. 12, UNION Agency – Science Press, February 2004.

C. Yuan, "Simultaneous Tracking of Multiple Objects for Augmented Reality Applications", *EG Multimedia Workshop*, pp. 41-47, Eurographics Association, 2004.

F.Liarokapis, S. Sylaiou, A.Basu, N.Mourkoussis, M.White, P.F.Lister, "An Interactive Visualisation Interface for Virtual Museums", VAST 2004: *The 5th International Symposium on Virtual Reality, Archaeology and Cultural Heritage*, pp. 47-56, Eurographics Association, 2004.

V. Vlahakis, A. Demiris, E. Bounos, N. Ioannidis, "A Novel Approach to Context-Sensitive Guided e-Tours in Cultural Sites: "Light" Augmented Reality on PDAs", *VAST 2004: The 5th International Symposium on Virtual Reality, Archaeology and Cultural Heritage*, pp. 57-66, Eurographics Association, 2004.

Nassir Navab, "Developing Killer Apps for Industrial Augmented Reality", *j-IEEE-CGA*, 24 (3), pp. 16-20, May /June 2004.

C. Dehais, M. Douze, G. Morin, V. Charvillat, "Augmented reality through real-time tracking of video sequences using a panoramic view", *International Conference on Pattern Recognition*, p. IV: 995-998, 2004.

Y. K. Yu, K. H. Wong, M. M. Y. Chang, "A fast and robust simultaneous pose tracking and structure recovery algorithm for augmented reality applications", *International Conference on Image Processing*, p. II: 1029-1032, 2004.

Printed in January 2011

GANGEMI EDITORE SPA – ROMA

www.gangemieditore.it